M000169344

# The Real Food Real People Cook Book

The
Real Food
Real People
Cook Book

First published in 2007 by
Appletree Press Ltd.
The Old Potato Station
14 Howard Street South
Belfast BT17 1AP

Tel: +44 (0) 28 90 243074
Fax: +44 (0) 28 90 246756

Website: www.appletree.ie
Email: reception@appletree.ie

Copyright © Appletree Press 2007

The Real People Cookbook

Acknowledgements

This book and my involvement with this special project were
made possible by a group of very hard working people whom
I would like to thank. The ever smiling Louise Oakes, Gillian
Holland and Louise Hegarty from Creative Solutions with
their design team John Conway and Tom Thornbury. Evelyn
Moynihan, Des O'Mahony and Carl Miles who work tirelessly
behind the scenes in SuperValu marketing. My agent Borra
Garson. Our immensely patient and fun loving food photographer
Harry Weir and the lovely Alberto Peroli who took the photos
of me. Our food stylists Sally Dunne and Sharon Hearne-Smith.
Rachel Sherry, Caroline Moody, Anna Murphy and their team
in Grayling who worked so hard to get photos of our wonderful
winners. Chefs Phelim Byrne, Aongus Hanly, Domini Kemp and
Hugh McNally who gave some gorgeous recipes of their own. To
all of our stores and their winners who make the recipes in this
book simply jump off the pages. And finally John Murphy, Mark
Elliott, Jim Black and their team in Appletree Press who pulled
the whole thing together so beautifully.

Clodagh McKenna

# The Real Food Real People Cook Book

Compiled by Clodagh McKenna, featuring winning recipes from SuperValu Shoppers nationwide

# The Real Food Real People Cook Book

The book that you're holding in your hands is a collection of the winning recipes in the SuperValu Real Food Recipe Competition. These recipes have been submitted by very talented amateur cooks from all over the country, and their entries are a combination of their own personal creations, or unique twists on old favourites.

Remember though, when using this book, that these recipes have been written by our winners in the way that reflects how they cook them at home. Because of this, the recipes aren't necessarily in the standardised way that you might find in those written by a professional chef or cookery writer. So approaches to timings, temperatures, measurements, and even utensils may differ from recipe to recipe. In other words if you're unsure you should use your own discretion when trying them at home to make sure that you're always happy with the end result. The best bit about all of this is that you're guaranteed the adventure that should always come when cooking and trying new things in your kitchen at home, so enjoy this glimpse into how others do it.

# CONTENTS

The
Real **Food**
Real **People**
Cook Book

**THE REAL FOOD PROGRAMME - OVERALL WINNER**
Page 15

**BRUNCH & LIGHT SNACKS**
Page 16

**MEAT**
Page 38

**POULTRY**
Page 72

**FISH**
Page 96

**VEGETABLES**
Page 124

**BAKING & TREATS**
Page 148

**DESSERTS**
Page 176

A very
**special recipe book**
from SuperValu

Dear Reader,

I'd like to take this opportunity to thank you for purchasing this book, and to tell you a little about why SuperValu decided to initiate this very special project. At the heart of SuperValu is real food and real people and in Ireland real food, cooked by real people is part of our culture and our heritage. We came up with this book because we wanted to celebrate this love of food and in doing so take the opportunity to give something back to the community.

This book is special in that it contains recipes sent in by you – real food, by real people. We put a call out through our stores, and the response was overwhelming. Bringing in the help of well known chef, Clodagh McKenna, we have selected recipes for every occasion. What makes this book even more special, however, is that for every one of our stores represented by a recipe in this book, we will make a contribution to the charity of their choice. This means that the proceeds from each and every book we sell will go directly to the communities you know and care about, communities in which we all have our part to play. You can see the charities that are benefiting throughout the book – just look out for them on the different recipe pages.

Clodagh herself is well known for her passionate commitment to cooking with local, seasonal produce from suppliers you can know and trust. As that is a commitment we share at SuperValu, we are delighted to be working with her on this project. At each and every one of our locally-owned stores, retailers take pride and care in selecting the best, freshest produce and bringing it to you. We also take pride in caring for and serving our shoppers, as well as the communities of which we are a part. You will see these fresh, locally sourced products in all of our recipes which include everything from light snacks and main courses to traditional Irish favourites and delicious desserts.

I hope you enjoy this book and the food it inspires; maybe you have contributed a recipe, maybe you know someone who has. Perhaps you will find new favourite meals, or be reminded of dishes you used to enjoy but haven't made for a while. Whatever you choose to make, you can be assured that you'll find the very best ingredients to prepare it at your local SuperValu store.

On behalf of all of us at SuperValu, I'd like to thank all of you once again. I wish you a great many enjoyable meals and send my best regards to your chosen charities and to your own local communities.

A **feast** of **real food**
from your
favourite recipes

Nothing beats the taste of good food, locally produced, mouthwateringly fresh, and cooked with love and a little bit of skill. Reading these recipes, I can see that so many of you agree. From baked chicken with chorizo, to the lightness of smoked mackerel pâté; from Guinness stew, to a luxurious cáca milis; these dishes will really tickle your taste buds . And they taste all the better knowing that with each copy of this book sold, a contribution is going to your local SuperValu's chosen charity.

Some of these recipes are family favourites, handed down from mother to daughter (and also fathers to sons!); while others are clever adaptations of those memorable meals we've all enjoyed abroad on holidays. I've been thrilled with the inventiveness and variety you've brought to preparing great meals — and I've even picked up some tips from you myself. I've also added some of my own favourites to the mix, as well as some recipes from a few chefs you may know from your own part of the country; Phelim Byrne from Wexford, Domini Kemp from Dublin, Aongus Hanly from Dublin and Hugh McNally from Clare, so within the pages of this book, you're assured of a feast for any occasion.

The recipes are all simple to follow; some have an emphasis on healthy eating, some are adventurous, and some are sheer indulgence; but the best thing about them for me is that they encourage you to get out there and experiment with the wonderful fresh and local produce you'll find on your nearest SuperValu shelves. As you go through the book, look out for seasonal favourites, when you're assured that our own locally grown foods will taste their best. Try a fresh summer salad to make the most of the red ripe tomatoes bursting with summer sun, or later in the year, poached pears with cinnamon and red wine are a warming autumn treat.

Putting this book together has been inspiring, and I'm really encouraged that as a nation we're starting to cook again. It is a fantastic skill to pass on to your children and a wonderful way to bring people together, as family and friends sit down round a table to share great food. When I walk down SuperValu aisles and see a Gubbeen cheese, a Cashel Blue, or any number of locally produced foodstuffs, I feel a real sense of pride for our farmers and growers. When we buy locally produced food from our own local Irish shops, we are preserving age old traditions of food production and farming; and when we cook them to favourite recipes, we're also keeping family traditions alive - as well as creating some new ones.

These recipes are easy to prepare, using gorgeous ingredients and I can assure you that with them you can produce fantastic meals. Enjoy them!

*Clodagh McKenna*

# Sinead Clarke's Baked Chicken with Chorizo

## Meet our overall winner, Sinead Clarke from Swords

My own concoction — quick and easy recipe to prepare, especially if you're a busy mom. And it's totally yummy!

Serves: 4
Preparation time: 15 minutes
Cooking time: 45 minutes

**1 Red Onion**
**1 Red Pepper**
**1 Tin of Chickpeas, drained and rinsed**
**2-3 inches of Chorizo, sliced**
**4 Part boned Chicken Breasts, skin on**
**Paprika**
**Salt and Pepper**
**Glass of white wine or water**
**Parsley to garnish**

Slice the onion and pepper.

Place both in a casserole dish along with the chickpeas and sliced Chorizo.

Score the chicken using a knife and rub with a generous sprinkling of paprika.

Sit the chicken on top of the vegetable mixture and season with salt and pepper

Add the wine (or water) and bake in a preheated oven for 45 minutes at 180°C/350°F/gas 4.

Garnish with parsley and serve with potatoes or rice.

O'CIOBHAIN'S SUPERVALU, SWORDS
NOMINATED LOCAL CHARITY: DOWN SYNDROME IRELAND

# Brunch and light snacks

Recipes

# Clodagh McKenna's Homemade Muesli

Serves: 12
Preparation time: 5 minutes
Cooking time: 15 minutes

**300g jumbo oats**
**180g mixed nuts (almonds, hazelnuts, walnuts)**
**100g dried figs**
**100g dried apricots**
**70g dried cranberries**
**50g pumpkin seeds**
**50g sunflower seeds**

Spread the jumbo oats out on a large roasting tin and place in a preheated oven at 190°C for 15 minutes or until golden.

Then tip into a large bowl and allow to cool.

Roughly chop the dried fruits and nuts and add into the bowl, with the seeds. Mix well.

Transfer to an airtight container and serve for breakfast with some natural yoghurt or milk.

DEDICATED TO:DONOHOE'S SUPERVALU, BALLYCONNELL
NOMINATED LOCAL CHARITY: LOCAL TIDY TOWNS
COMMITTEE

# Clodagh McKenna's Ardsallagh and Sundried Tomato Sausages

Serves: 4-6
Preparation time: 15 minutes
Cooking time: 10 minutes

**6 semi sundried tomatoes**
**450g minced free range pork, from neck or shoulder**
**50g Ardsallagh soft goats cheese**
**1 tbsp of dried oregano**
**1 free-range egg, beaten**
**salt and freshly ground pepper**
**olive oil**

Chop up the semi sundried tomatoes finely and place in a mixing bowl, with the minced pork, soft goats cheese, dried oregano and egg. Season with salt and pepper – mix well.

Then, divide the mixture into 10 pieces and roll each one into a sausage shape.

Heat a frying pan and add a dollop of olive oil – one by one add in the sausages and gently cook for about 10 minutes, turning every couple of minutes to make sure they are evenly cooked.

DEDICATED TO:BYRNE'S SUPERVALU, ASTON QUAY, DUBLIN
NOMINATED LOCAL CHARITY: LOCAL MEALS ON WHEELS

# Rosemary Cooney's Canadian Mountie Brunch

A Canadian colleague introduced me to this dish many years ago. Now we always have it on Christmas Day as a special treat!

Serves: 4
Preparation time: 15 minutes
Cooking time: 40 - 45 minutes

**8 slices of white bread, crusts removed**
**4 slices of back bacon**
**4 slices of cheddar cheese**
**3 eggs**
**½ teaspoon dried mustard**
**1 shallot, diced**
**1 teaspoon Worcestershire sauce**
**1½ cups of milk**
**dash of Tabasco (optional)**
**25g butter**
**crushed cornflakes**
**pinch of salt and pepper**

Grease a baking dish and cover the bottom with four slices of bread.

Cover with bacon and a slice of cheese.

Then cover with remaining four slices of bread (to make sandwiches).

Beat the eggs with the salt and pepper.

Add the mustard, onion, pepper, Worcestershire sauce, milk and Tabasco to the eggs.

Pour this mixture over the sandwiches in the dish

Cover this and leave it in the fridge overnight

In the morning remove from fridge, melt the butter and pour it over the top of the mixture. Then cover with a layer of cornflakes.

Bake this at 180°C for 35-40 minutes.

Remove from the oven and leave to sit for 10 minutes before serving

# Noreen Harrington's Blue Cheese, Pear and Bacon

I serve this as a breakfast in our guesthouse. It's my signature dish and guests love it!

Serves: 1
Preparation time: 5 minutes
Cooking time: 5 minutes

**2 slices of ciabatta bread**
**1 sweet ripe pear**
**2 slices of Cashel Blue cheese (from a block)**
**2 streaky rashers of bacon**
**sweet chutney to serve**

Toast the ciabatta lightly.

Slice the pear and place on top of the toast. Cover with Cashel Blue cheese.

Pop under a preheated grill until the cheese is bubbling, taking care not to burn.

Grill the rashers until crisp and place these on top of the cheese.

Serve with sweet chutney.

MURPHY'S SUPERVALU, KENMARE
NOMINATED LOCAL CHARITY: KENMARE HOSPITAL

# Breda McCarthy's Breakfast Surprise

This is a lovely alternative to bacon and eggs, or it can be great comfort food for supper. Children love the 'surprise' in the centre!

Serves: 2
Preparation time: 30 minutes
Cooking time: 30 minutes

**2 large free range eggs**
**4 oz breadcrumbs**
**1 oz good strong cheddar cheese, grated**
**1 oz melted butter**
**4 rashers**

**For the Béchamel Sauce:**
**½ pint full fat milk**
**1½ oz butter**
**2 level tbsp sieved white flour**
**a pinch of nutmeg**
**salt and white pepper**

**Optional Extra:**
**½ bay leaf, sprig of parsley, 1 sliced carrot, ¼ small onion wrapped in muslin and secured with string**

Preheat oven to 230°C/450°F/Gas 8.

In a small pan bring some water to simmering point. Gently place eggs in the pan and leave for 3 minutes at a gentle simmer (4 minutes if eggs just out of fridge).

Cook rashers under the grill until crispy, drain and chop into small pieces.

Remove the eggs and place in cold water, then carefully peel off shells.

To make the Béchamel sauce: Gently melt butter, remove from heat and stir in the sieved white flour until amalgamated.

Heat milk and gradually add this to the butter/flour mixture until it thickens. Return to heat stirring until it comes to simmering point.

Before adding to the butter/flour, if you wish you can simmer the muslin parcels of seasoning in the milk for a few minutes and remove before adding to the butter/flour mix – it gives a lovely extra dimension to the sauce.

At this point reduce heat to its lowest point and leave sauce to cook for 10 minutes, stirring regularly. Add salt, pepper and nutmeg, taste and adjust seasoning if necessary.

Place the chopped rashers in the bottom of a ramekin dish. Carefully place an egg in each dish on top of the rashers, and pour the Béchamel sauce over the egg.

Mix breadcrumbs with grated cheese and place on top of sauce. Then pour melted butter over the breadcrumbs.

Place in the top of a very hot oven for 4-5 minutes until top is crisp and golden.

Serve immediately.

CAULFIELDS'S SUPERVALU, WATERFORD
NOMINATED LOCAL CHARITY: LIONS CLUB

# Mairead Finnegan's Three Cheese Frittata

We love to cook frittatas as a weekend brunch using left over potatoes. Delicious hot or cold.

Serves: 4
Preparation time: 15 minutes
Cooking time: 25 minutes

**8 large free range eggs**
**4 medium sized potatoes – cooked, peeled and cubed**
**8 cherry tomatoes, halved**
**3 spring onions**
**75g feta cheese**
**100g grated red cheddar and mozzarella**
**1 tbsp olive oil**
**25g butter**
**salt and ground black pepper**

In a large bowl beat the eggs with a whisk.

In a large pan heat the butter and olive oil, add the cubed potatoes and cook gently for about 5 minutes. Add salt and pepper to the egg mixture, add the spring onions, chopped tomatoes, and crumble in the feta cheese.

Pour this mixture into the pan and cook over a low to medium heat. After about 10 minutes the frittata will begin to set.

Sprinkle the top with cheddar and mozzarella.

Remove from heat and place under a moderate grill for 10 minutes or until cooked on top.

Can be enjoyed hot or cold, whichever you prefer.

O'BRIEN'S SUPERVALU, KELLS
NOMINATED LOCAL CHARITY: ST VINCENT DE PAUL

# Emer McNamara's Boxty

This was always mum's favourite. Boxty is a real traditional Irish dish, and unique to Ireland. The outside of Boxty should be crispy, the inside just cooked!

Serves: 4
Preparation time: 10 minutes
Cooking time: 10 minutes

**1lb uncooked floury potatoes**
**6 oz/175g plain flour**
**¾ tsp salt**
**4 oz/100g grated cheese (optional)**

Peel and grate the potatoes.

Add the flour and salt, and mix.

Roll out the mixture to about 1½ cm thick and cut into your preferred shape.

Cook these slowly, in a little butter, on a hot pan until well browned.

Turn over and cook the other side.

Serve hot with a sprinkle of grated cheese and butter.

Tip

Traditionally Boxty was fried in bacon fat for breakfast. If you plan to do this it's a good idea to make each piece thicker, and slice in two horizontally before cooking.

SWEENEY'S SUPERVALU, ACHILL SOUND
NOMINATED LOCAL CHARITY: ACHILL BRANCH OF CROÍ

# Helen Shanahan's Fresh Tomato Salad

I once bought too many tomatoes and this was a great way to use them up. Simple and fresh this is delicious on its own, or as an accompaniment.

Serves: 4
Preparation time: 10 minutes
(Plus standing time 1 hour)

**5 large ripe tomatoes, cut into thick slices**
**1 small red onion, thinly sliced**
**4 tbsp of extra virgin olive oil**
**1 tbsp balsamic vinegar**
**salt and pepper**
**4 oz feta cheese, crumbled**
**2 oz black olives**
**1 tbsp chopped fresh parsley**

Arrange sliced tomatoes on a serving dish and top with onion slices. Drizzle with oil and vinegar and sprinkle with salt and pepper.

Allow to stand for 1 hour at room temperature.

Sprinkle with cheese, olives and parsley and serve.

Tip

Replace parsley with fresh chopped basil leaves and the feta with buffalo mozzarella. This makes a great accompaniment to a barbecue.

DOLAN'S SUPERVALU, CAHIR
NOMINATED LOCAL CHARITY: LOCAL VINCENT DE PAUL AND MEALS ON WHEELS

# Claire Cooke's Tasty Coeliac Pizza

We love pizza in our house, as one of the family is a coeliac we make our own bases. Read on, it's really not that scary and not just for coeliacs!

Serves: 4,
Preparation time: 20 minutes (Although the bases take a bit of practise, I won't lie to you, but totally worth it!),
Cooking time: 20 minutes

**500g Gluten free flour (Odlums Tritamyl flour)**
**1 sachet of easy blend yeast (Don't be scared!)**
**1 tsp of sugar**
**A little salt**
**Some dried mixed herbs (optional)**
**400ml of warm water (microwave for 1½ minutes)**

Mix all the dry ingredients together in a mixing bowl.

Add warm water and mix to a soft dough with a wooden spoon. Divide into 4 portions and knead each on a floured surface (a few quick turns and folds will do, nothing too energetic!).

At this point you can either roll your dough for thin and crispy, or just squash it out for deep dish and chewy.

Pizza bases should be laid out on to baking sheets lined with baking parchment and are ready for dressing.

Depending on how industrious/chilled out/stressed you are you can make your own sauce by softening a chopped onion in some olive oil, add a tin of tomatoes, a crushed clove of garlic, some sugar and basil.

Simmer this for 10 minutes and the pureé it. Alternatively you can use a jar of SuperValu pasta sauce (which is also gluten free!).

After that it's all down to personal taste – add your favourite toppings and cook in the oven for 20 minutes at 180°C. Mine is the 'Janeymac, what are you putting on that' version – cheddar, mozzarella, pepperoni, vegetables and pineapple! Delicious!

Top Tip: Dip the crusts in garlic butter or pesto. Saturday night bliss!

KANE'S SUPERVALU, DONABATE
NOMINATED LOCAL CHARITY: IRISH CANCER SOCIETY

# Ann Kearney's Baked Mushrooms with Bacon and Onion

This is a favourite starter in our house, or sometimes a delicious lunchtime treat! Quick and easy to prepare, it's always a winner.

Serves: 4
Preparation time: 10 minutes
Cooking time: 15 - 20 minutes

**4 large flat mushrooms**
**1 tbsp crème fraîche**
**3 tbsp breadcrumbs**
**1 onion, chopped**
**4 slices streaky bacon, chopped**
**butter and a little oil for frying**

Sauté onion and bacon together.

When cooked, combine these with the breadcrumbs and a large spoon of crème fraîche.

Remove the stem from the mushrooms and spoon the mixture into the resulting hollow.

Cook under the grill for 15-20 minutes.

KAVANAGH'S SUPERVALU, CASTLEBAR
NOMINATED LOCAL CHARITY: BRIGHT EYES

# Charles Stratton's Toad in the Hole

This is an old classic recipe which is sure to get mouths watering!

Serves: 4
Preparation time: 5 minutes
Cooking time: 35 - 40 minutes

**1 lb spicy sausages**
**1 cup self raising flour**
**pinch of salt**
**1 egg**
**½ pint milk**
**1 oz cooking fat**

Preheat the oven to 250°C. Cook the sausages in a medium sized roasting tin for 8-10 minutes until golden.

Make the batter by mixing the flour, salt and egg together and then slowly adding the milk until the mixture is a pourable solution.

When the sausages are cooked add the fat to the dish; when the fat is hot pour the batter mixture over the sausages.

Cook for 25-30 minutes until the batter has risen and is golden brown.

Serve with new potatoes, vegetables and gravy.

TWOHIG'S SUPERVALU, ABBEYFEALE
NOMINATED LOCAL CHARITY: THE AISLING GROUP

# Mary Cullinan's Sausage Plait

Delicious whether served hot or cold!

Serves: 4-6
Preparation time: 20 - 30 minutes
Cooking time: 30 - 40 minutes

**½ lb sausage meat**
**1 large onion, peeled and finely chopped**
**2 tbsp chopped parsley**
**pinch of mixed herbs**
**2 large hard boiled eggs, sliced**
**2 medium tomatoes, skinned and sliced**
**beaten egg or milk to glaze**

Mix the sausage meat, onion, parsley and mixed herbs together

Make up a shortcrust pastry either to your own recipe, or use a prepared pastry from SuperValu.

Roll out to a 12" square and place on a large baking sheet (ideally larger than the pastry).

Place half of the sausage meat down the centre of the pastry leaving a 4" space on either side of the filling.

Cover the sausage meat with the sliced eggs, and place the remaining sausage meat on top.

Cover with tomatoes.

Then cut diagonal ½" strips on each side of the filling. Take each strip separately and plait across the filling, alternating each side. Tuck in ends to neaten

For best results allow the sausage plait to relax for ½ hour before baking. Brush with glaze.

Bake in a preheated oven at 190°C/375°F/Gas 5 for 30-40 minutes.

MOLLOY'S SUPERVALU, ASHBOURNE
NOMINATED LOCAL CHARITY: LOCAL MEALS ON WHEELS

# Teri Ryan's Warm Chicken Salad

This is a combination of lots of my favourite summer salad recipes.

Serves: 4
Preparation time: 20 minutes
Cooking time: 10 minutes

**4 skinless chicken breasts**
**3 tbsp honey**
**1 clove garlic, crushed**
**1 tbsp sunflower oil**
**mixed lettuce (iceberg, gem, rocket) washed and dried**
**punnet of baby tomatoes**
**1 avocado peeled and diced**
**5 radishes**
**1 small cucumber, peeled and sliced**
**handful of halved walnuts and cashew nuts**

**Dressing:**
**8 tbsp olive oil**
**1 tbsp balsamic vinegar**
**1 tsp Dijon mustard**
**pinch of salt and freshly ground black pepper**

Cube the chicken breasts and place in a dish.

Drizzle with honey and allow to stand for 10 minutes.

Wash and dry lettuce and place in a serving bowl.

Prepare cucumber, radishes, tomatoes, walnuts, avocado and toss with the lettuce.

Heat the sunflower oil and fry the garlic until golden.

Add the chicken and any excess honey.

Cook until well browned and nutty looking. Add to the salad.

Make the salad dressing by combining all ingredients together.

Generously add the salad dressing to the salad and serve with crusty bread or warmed rolls.

MORIARTY'S SUPERVALU, BALBRIGGAN
NOMINATED LOCAL CHARITY: LOCAL MEALS ON WHEELS

# Amanda McCoy's Spinach Salad

First tried this salad on holiday in Florida, where they used oranges fresh from the tree.

Serves: 4
Preparation time: 5 minutes

**10 oz caster sugar**
**1 tsp mustard powder**
**1 tsp salt**
**250 ml vegetable or sunflower oil**
**150 ml red wine vinegar**
**1 red onion, chopped**
**½ tsp poppy seeds**
**2 mandarin oranges, chopped**
**1 bag baby spinach leaves**
**1 bag toasted flaked almonds**

Mix caster sugar, mustard powder, salt and oil and vinegar.

Put into blender for a few seconds.

Add chopped onion, poppy seeds and one of the mandarin oranges.

Blend all for 30 seconds - 1 minute.

Put baby spinach leaves in bowl, add almonds and remaining chopped orange pieces.

Pour dressing over this and serve.

SUPERVALU, LETTERKENNY
NOMINATED LOCAL CHARITY: DONEGAL HOSPICE

# Lynne Hyland's Chicken Avocado Salad

My husband recently came up with this recipe to add a nice twist to a normal salad.

Serves: 4 as a starter, 2 as a main
Preparation time: 10 minutes
Cooking time: 15 - 20 minutes

**2 chicken breasts**
**olive oil**
**1 pack of pancetta or bacon cubes**
**1 bag of mixed lettuce leaves**
**2 avocados, sliced**
**2 fresh vine tomatoes, chopped**
**good quality balsamic vinegar**
**salt and pepper**

Fry chicken in olive oil until cooked through.

When cooked, slice the chicken and leave aside to cool.

Meanwhile fry the pancetta/bacon.

In a large bowl tear up the lettuce, mix in the avocado, tomato and chicken.

Next crumble in the pancetta or bacon cubes.

Drizzle with olive oil and balsamic vinegar to taste

Season with salt and pepper and serve with fresh bread.

GILLESPIE'S SUPERVALU, BALTINGLASS
NOMINATED LOCAL CHARITY:
WEST WICKLOW DAY CARE CENTRE

# Chef Phelim Byrne's
# Mushroom and Smoked Bacon Pâté on Crisp Toasts

These tasty delights are perfect little starters or appetisers!

Serves: 6
Preparation time: 10 minutes plus chilling time (approx 2 hours)
Cooking time: 5 minutes

**1 large white onion, chopped**
**1 clove garlic, finely chopped**
**350g of assorted mushrooms**
**25g butter**
**1 tbsp sunflower oil**
**2 tbsp chopped herbs (parsley, chives, tarragon)**
**4 smoked bacon rashers, cooked**
**2 tbsp of cream cheese**
**salt and freshly ground black pepper**
**hot buttered toasts to serve**

Sauté the onion, garlic and mushrooms in a hot pan with the butter and oil for 4-5 minutes until coloured.

Season the mix well, then add the chopped fresh herbs and pop into a food processor with the cooked bacon.

Proceed to blend to achieve a relatively smooth mix.

Allow to cool, then add in the cream cheese and mix well. Refrigerate for at least 2 hours.

Serve the cooled pâté on hot buttered toasts – delicious!

DEDICATED TO: GARVEY'S SUPERVALU, DUNGARVAN
NOMINATED LOCAL CHARITY: FRIENDS OF ST. JOSEPH'S
HOSPICE, DUNGARVAN

# Kit Cummin's Lambs Liver Pâté

Wow your guests with this simple yet impressive dinner party starter. Delicious!

Serves: 8
Preparation time: 15 minutes
Cooking time: 10 minutes

**1lb lambs liver, chopped**
**4 bacon rashers**
**6 mushrooms, finely chopped**
**2 cloves garlic, finely chopped**
**1 onion, finely chopped**
**½ glass chicken stock**
**dash of brandy (optional)**

Fry lambs liver for approx 5 minutes.

Add rashers, mushrooms, garlic, onion and fry for a few more minutes.

Add the stock and brandy (if using) and cook for 4-5 minutes (ensuring bacon and liver are cooked through).

Transfer to a liquidiser and liquidise for 3 minutes or until smooth.

Pour into ramekin dishes and allow to cool.

Cover and refrigerate until needed (This also freezes very well).

Serve with toast or brown bread.

TREACY'S SUPERVALU, CHURCHTOWN
NOMINATED LOCAL CHARITY: THE AISLING GROUP

# Blánaid O'Brien's Avocado Pâté with Lime and Crispy Bacon

I used to make this a lot when I lived in London. I have revised it several times since.

Serves: 4
Preparation time: 15 minutes
Cooking time: 15 minutes

**2 avocados, firm not overly ripe**
**4 boiled eggs (omega eggs with omega 3**
 **would be my choice), finely chopped**
**2 tbsp red wine vinegar**
**1 clove garlic, chopped**
**juice ½ lime (reserve other half for serving)**
**2 slices crispy bacon, diced**
**Sea salt and some freshly milled black pepper**
**rocket leaves or lettuce**
**SuperValu crusty white rolls**

Cut avocados in half and remove stones, save the skins for later. Remove flesh and mix with eggs, vinegar, garlic and lime juice.

Taste. Season with salt and black pepper if required, taste again.

Spoon the avocado mixture back into the avocado skins and sprinkle with crispy bacon.

Serve on a bed of rocket or lettuce with a slice of lime and crusty bread.

Enjoy!

Avocado doesn't hang around so it's best served immediately. Perfect as a starter, Sunday brunch or supper.

TARPEY'S SUPERVALU, CAVAN
NOMINATED LOCAL CHARITY: CAVAN PARISH DRUGS AWARENESS

# Michele O'Reilly's Lentil and Bacon Soup

Quick and easy to make, and the kids love it!

Serves: 6
Preparation time: 15 minutes
Cooking time: 90 - 100 minutes

**8 oz red split lentils**
**6 pints of cold water**
**8 large potatoes, peeled and quartered**
**2 large onions, chopped**
**8 slices bacon**
**salt and pepper**

Put the lentils into a large pot and add 6 pints of water.

Add salt and pepper, cover with lid and bring to the boil.

Meanwhile, peel and quarter the potatoes and add to the pot.

Chop the onions and add to the pot.

Bring back to the boil, stirring from time to time.

Once boiled, lower heat and allow to simmer.

Remove the fat from the bacon and chop into strips.

Add to the pot and simmer for 40-50 minutes until the potatoes are soft.

If you prefer a smoother consistency whiz in a food processor to your requirements.

Serve with fresh crusty bread.

DUNPHY'S SUPERVALU, GRANARD
NOMINATED LOCAL CHARITY: ST CHRISTOPHER'S, LONGFORD

# Louise Fearnside's Asparagus and Ham Bake

This can be served as a starter or supper dish. It's a handy and quick recipe which I made up one day and have been making ever since.

Serves: 6
Preparation time: 10 minutes
Cooking time: 30 - 35 minutes

**bunch fresh asparagus**
**½ pint fresh milk**
**2 oz butter**
**1 tbsp plain flour**
**2 oz grated cheddar**
**6 slices ham from deli counter**
**2 oz fresh parmesan optional**
**salt and pepper to season**

Trim and discard the woody ends from the asparagus. Cook in boiling water until tender (2-3 minutes).

Meanwhile, melt butter and add flour, then slowly stir in milk.

Add grated cheese stir until melted. Season to taste. Bring to the boil and reduce to simmer for 6-7 minutes, stirring until thickened.

Divide asparagus into 6 bunches and wrap in the ham.

Place in oven proof dish and cover with cheese sauce. Bake at 180°C for 20-25 minutes until golden brown. Sprinkle with parmesan if desired and serve.

GARVEY'S SUPERVALU, CORBALLY
NOMINATED LOCAL CHARITY: MILFORD HOSPICE

# Meat

Recipes

# Clodagh McKenna's Filet Mignon with a Red Wine, Rosemary and Garlic jus

Serves: 2
Preparation time: 2-3 minutes
Cooking time: 10 minutes

**2 x filet mignon**
**1 x knob of unsalted butter**
**1 x cup of red wine**
**2 x cloves of garlic, crushed**
**1 tsp of freshly chopped rosemary**
**salt and freshly ground black pepper**

Season the filet mignon with salt and pepper.

Place a frying pan or skillet over a high heat - add the butter. When it has melted add the filet mignons.

Cook on each side for 3 minutes for medium rare. Remove from the pan to rest, and then add the red wine, garlic and rosemary to the pan.

Leave to reduce by half and then drizzle over the filet mignon or serve in a jug.

DEDICATED TO: ARTHUR'S SUPERVALU, CARLOW
NOMINATED LOCAL CHARITY: HOLY ANGELS, CARLOW

# Marie Duggan's Pizza Irlanda

We make pizzas every Saturday evening. We experiment with new toppings all the time too. This is one of our yummiest!

Serves: 4
Preparation time: 20 minutes (plus 2 hours for dough to rise)
Cooking time: 12 minutes

**Pizza Base:**
**400g strong white flour**
**100ml olive oil**
**350ml warm water**
**7g (1 sachet) fast action bread yeast**
**pinch of salt**

**Pizza Toppings:**
**Few tablespoons of Loyd Grossman pasta sauce**
**6 slices of Clonakilty black pudding (cooked)**
**3 Clonakilty pork sausages (cooked and sliced)**
**1 eating apple, thinly sliced**
**4 tbsp grated cheddar and mozzarella cheese**
**pinch of sugar**

Put dry pizza ingredients together in a bowl and then add all of the olive oil, mix these ingredients with your hands until it has a breadcrumb-like texture.

Now add the 350ml of water a little at a time. You should end up with a ball of dough that's not too sticky!

Place the ball of dough on a floured work surface and knead it for about 10 minutes.

Put a small drop of olive oil in a large bowl, place the kneaded dough in the bowl, cover with cling film and cover that with a tea towel. Leave it for 2 hours to let the dough rise.

Meanwhile prepare the toppings; fry/grill and slice the black puddings and sausages.

Don't forget to set the oven now to 200°C!

Peel and slice the apple and sauté the slices in a small pan for 5 minutes with a little butter, a drop of lemon juice and a pinch of sugar.

When the dough is ready (risen), divide the large dough ball into 4 smaller balls of dough.

Roll each thinly and place on a pizza tray.

Top the pizza with some of the pasta sauce.

Then spread the sausage slices over the pizza, add the black pudding slices (or alternatively crumble this over the pizza) and scatter the caramelised apple over the pizza. Finally top with the cheese.

Bake in the oven for approximately 12 minutes.

KYNE'S SUPERVALU, MOYCULLEN
NOMINATED LOCAL CHARITY: VOICES FOR GALWAY

# Karena Cahill's Spaghetti and Meatballs with Egg on top

This is an alternative twist on the traditional spaghetti and meatballs – delicious!

Serves: 4
Preparation time: 15 minutes
Cooking time: 40 minutes

**For the meatballs:**
500g/1lb 2oz minced beef or lamb
1 onion, very finely chopped
3 cloves garlic, crushed
1 tsp ground ginger
1 tsp ground cumin
½ tsp chilli powder
1 tsp paprika
1 small handful fresh coriander leaves, finely chopped
1 small handful fresh flatleaf parsley, finely chopped
1 egg yolk
salt and pepper

1 packet of spaghetti

**For the sauce:**
2 tbsp olive oil
1 small onion, finely chopped
2 tbsp tomato purée
400g/14oz can chopped tomatoes, drained of excess juice
2 tsp honey
200g/7oz frozen peas
4 free-range eggs
chopped fresh parsley, to garnish

For the meatballs, place the minced beef or lamb, onion, garlic, spices, fresh herbs, egg yolk and some salt and pepper into a large bowl.

Use your hands to mix all the ingredients together until well combined. Shape into walnut-sized balls and set aside.

For the sauce, heat the olive oil in a frying pan or heavy-bottomed casserole dish. Add the onion and cook slowly over a low heat until translucent.

Increase the heat to medium-high, add the meatballs and brown lightly.

Stir the tomato purée into the chopped tomatoes then add to the dish with the honey.

Stir gently, cover and simmer for 10 minutes.

Stir in the peas, then break the eggs on top of the stew, turn the heat right down and cook with the lid on for about ten minutes, or until the eggs are cooked to your liking.

Sprinkle over the chopped parsley and serve with cooked spaghetti.

# Pauline Wilson's Dairy Free Lasagne

One of my daughters is lactose intolerant so I developed this milk free variation of traditional lasagne for her. The rest of the family now prefer it too and it's a real favourite!

Serves: 8 - 10
Preparation time: 20 minutes
Cooking time: 55-60 minutes

**For the meat sauce:**
**400g tin plum tomatoes**
**450g jar bolognese sauce**
**1 small glass red wine (optional)**
**1 tbsp olive oil (extra virgin)**
**1 clove garlic, finely chopped (or crushed)**
**1 large onion, finely chopped**
**1 carrot, finely chopped (optional)**
**500g steak mince**
**1 tbsp tomato purée**

**For the mushroom sauce:**
**3 tbsp olive oil (extra virgin)**
**250g fresh mushrooms**
**1 tbsp plain flour**
**1 pint soya milk or rice milk**

**500g box of dry lasagne sheets**

Preheat oven 200°C/ 400°C/ Gas 6
Put the plum tomatoes, jar of sauce, and wine (if using) into a medium sized pot. Bring to the boil and then leave to simmer. Heat oil in a separate pan, add the garlic, onion and carrot (if using) and fry over a medium heat for around 6-7 minutes. Add these to the pot of sauce. Using the same pan, brown the mince for a few minutes before adding to the sauce. Add the tomato purée and seasoning and leave to simmer while you make the mushroom sauce. Finely slice half of the mushrooms and fry them in 1 tablespoon of olive oil for 2-3 minutes until starting to brown. Lift out with a slotted spoon and leave to one side.

Chop the remaining mushrooms into very small pieces and fry lightly over a low heat in the remaining 2 tbsp of olive oil for 2-3 minutes. Sprinkle the flour over the mushrooms in the pan. Using a wooden spoon keep stirring the flour coated mushrooms for 1 minute. Remove from the heat; gradually add the soya milk, stirring all the time. Return to the heat, bring to the boil, stirring all the time until the sauce thickens. Add the reserved mushrooms to the pan of sauce. Season to taste.
Into a square oven proof dish, put a layer of the meat sauce, follow with a layer of lasagne sheets. Then meat sauce, mushroom sauce, lasagne and repeat. Finish off the top with a layer of mushroom sauce. Cover with tinfoil and cook in the oven for 35-40 minutes, until golden brown. Serve with fresh mixed salad and crusty bread.

KAVANAGH'S SUPERVALU, DUNGLOE
NOMINATED LOCAL CHARITY: DUNGLOE HYDROPOOL

# Marie McInerney's Nana's Stew

My Nana gave me this recipe 3 months before she passed away. I make this delicious stew for my 1 year old daughter who loves it. I am so proud that Nana gave me this opportunity to cook for her great-granddaughter.

Serves: 2
Preparation time: 10 minutes
Cooking time: 60 minutes

**1 lb lean beef or lamb pieces**
**1 tbsp olive oil**
**1 onion, finely chopped**
**1 tomato, finely chopped**
**1 clove of garlic, finely chopped**
**½ pint chicken stock**
**1 large potato, peeled and grated**
**salt and pepper**

Preheat the oven to 180°C/350°F/Gas 4

Fry the meat in olive oil until brown (about 3-4 minutes) and then transfer to a casserole dish. Fry the onion, tomato and garlic for 2-3 minutes until soft.

Next add the chicken stock and potato (this thickens the sauce). Taste, and season as required  Simmer for 5 minutes and then add to casserole dish.

Put the casserole dish in the oven for 40 - 50 minutes until the meat is tender.

Serve with creamed mashed potatoes and sliced carrots.

DANO'S SUPERVALU, MALLOW
NOMINATED LOCAL CHARITY: COPE MALLOW

# Chef Phelim Byrne's Slow Cooked Pork Belly, Honey Glazed Carrots

Serves: 6
Preparation time: 15 minutes + cooling time
Cooking time: 3 hours

**1 x 4lb pork belly, skin removed, and rolled**

**For the Stock:**
**vegetables: 1 carrot, 1 onion, 1 leek, 3 celery sticks**
**12 peppercorns**
**a sprig of thyme**
**zest of 1 orange and 1 lemon**
**3 tbsp honey**

**For the Honey Glazed Carrots:**
**400g baby carrots**
**salt and freshly ground black pepper**
**1 tbsp honey**
**25g unsalted butter**
**handful of sesame seeds**

Place the prepared rolled pork belly in a large pot, and add enough water to cover it. Add all the stock ingredients to the pot and bring to the boil. Next, reduce the heat to a gentle simmer and cook for 2-3 hours.

When cooked, allow to cool in the liquid, then remove the meat and cut into 6 equal portions. Place portions on a tray and drizzle with the honey. Bake these at 180°C until crisp and caramelised (Approximately 10-12 minutes). Meanwhile, boil the baby carrots in salted water until al dente, season and drizzle with honey and butter. Sprinkle these with sesame seeds.

Serve the pork on a bed of the carrots and enjoy!

DEDICATED TO: TWOHIG'S SUPERVALU, KANTURK
NOMINATED LOCAL CHARITY: KANTURK HOSPITAL

# Sylvia Crawford's Beef Goulash

A family favourite for parties. Just one pot, no mess and they'll all come back for more.

Serves: 4 - 6
Preparation time: 20 minutes
Cooking time: 2½ hours

**1½ lb steak**
**2 large onions, chopped**
**1 clove garlic, crushed**
**1 tbsp oil**
**1 tbsp flour**
**1 tbsp paprika**
**14 oz tin tomatoes**
**1 medium red or green pepper**
**5 fl oz sour cream**
**salt and pepper**

Brown cubes of meat in a hot pan. Remove and put aside.

Stir in onion and cook for 5 minutes until golden.

Add garlic and return meat to pan.

Sprinkle in flour and paprika and stir to soak up all juices.

Add tomatoes, pepper and salt and bring slowly to the boil.

Cover with lid and cook for 2 hours.

Stir in peppers and cook for a further 30 minutes.

Serve with rice or potatoes.

MURPHY'S SUPERVALU, NENAGH
NOMINATED LOCAL CHARITY: ST VINCENT DE PAUL

# Nessa Robins' Beef Stew with Red Wine and Cranberry

This is a very simple stew which is especially delicious on a cold winters day. Great when cranberries are in season!

Serves: 4
Preparation time: 15 minutes
Cooking time: 1 hour 40 minutes

**cup of flour**
**sea salt and black pepper**
**2 tbsp olive oil**
**2 lb sirloin steak, cubed**
**3 onions, sliced into rings**
**½ pint red wine**
**½ pint beef stock**
**3 tbsp cranberry sauce**
**handful of fresh cranberries**
**parsley to garnish**

Combine the flour with the salt and pepper.

Toss the steak in the seasoned flour.

Heat the oil in the pan and add the beef. Fry until brown and remove to a plate.

Add a little more oil and fry the onions.

Return the beef to the pan and then add the wine and stock.

Bring to the boil, then lower heat and simmer for 1½ hours.

Stir in the cranberry sauce and the cranberries and simmer for another 10 minutes.

Serve piping hot with creamy mash, green beans and a sprinkle of parsley.

BUCKLEY'S SUPERVALU, MOATE
NOMINATED LOCAL CHARITY: ST VINCENT DE PAUL

# Grett O'Connor's
# The Everyone Loves It Homemade Burger

From your fussy four-year-old to a diet-conscious granny, everyone will love this beef burger: guaranteed NO leftovers!

Serves: 3 adult sized burgers or lots of small ones!
Preparation time: 5 minutes
Cooking time: 30 minutes

**1lb steak mince**
**2 medium sized cooked potatoes, peeled and chopped into small pieces**
**1 large onion, chopped**
**1 tbsp soy sauce**
**2 tbsp mango chutney**
**1 egg**
**salt and pepper**
**a fistful of flour**

Put the beef, potatoes, onion, soy sauce, mango chutney, egg and salt and pepper into a large bowl.

With clean hands, mix the ingredients thoroughly, squishing them through your fingers so you get right through the meat.

Put a liberal dusting of flour on a chopping board and shape the mixture into burgers to your preferred size.

Lay them on a greased roasting pan and cook in a preheated oven 190°C for about 30 minutes.

Turn them at least twice during cooking.

Delicious served with a creamy pepper sauce!

O'LEARY'S SUPERVALU, MACROOM
NOMINATED LOCAL CHARITY: MACROOM HOSPITAL

# Chef Aongus Hanly's
# Grilled Marinated Gigot Lamb Chops

The simplest of flavours put together for this tasty marinade make Lamb Chops finger licking good!

Serves: 4
Preparation time: 10 minutes
Cooking time: 10 minutes

**8 gigot lamb chops**
**large sprig of rosemary, finely chopped**
**juice of 2 lemons**
**2 tbsp of olive oil**
**salt and pepper**

Mix together the chopped rosemary, lemon juice and olive oil.

In large mixing bowl toss the gigot chops and marinade together.

In a smaller container layer the chops, pour over the remaining marinade, cover and refrigerate over night.

Pre-heat the grill. Season the chops and grill them for 3-4 minutes on either side.

DEDICATED TO: DAVEY'S SUPERVALU, BALLYMOTE
NOMINATED LOCAL CHARITY: SLIGO HOSPICE

# Chef Phelim Byrne's Thai style beef and noodle stir fry

Serves: 4
Preparation time: 10 minutes, Cooking time: 10-15 minutes

**200g egg or rice noodles**
**300g beef steak, thinly sliced**
**3 tbsp vegetable oil**
**1 white onion, finely sliced**
**1 clove of garlic, finely chopped**
**½ tsp red Thai curry paste**
**1 red chilli**
**100 ml coconut milk**
**2 tbsp chopped coriander**
**1 tbsp crushed cashew nuts**
**salt and pepper**

First cook the noodles and strain, drizzle with 1 teaspoon of oil to prevent them sticking and leave to one side. Stir-fry the beef with 1 teaspoon of the oil in a very hot pan for 3-4 minutes and leave to one side.

Add the onions and garlic to the preheated frying pan and cook with the curry paste for 1-2 minutes over a medium heat with the remaining teaspoon of oil. Deseed and slice or finely chop the chilli and add to the mix along with the coconut milk.

Now add the noodles and stir fried beef combining all the ingredients.

Quickly mix in the chopped coriander and crushed cashew nuts and season to taste with salt and pepper. Enjoy!

*Tip: use a little nutty oil like sesame oil when the noodles are cooked for a better flavour and don't stir fry the beef for too long.*

DEDICATED TO: O'KEEFFE'S SUPERVALU, BOHERBUE
NOMINATED LOCAL CHARITY: COPE KANTURK AND ST JOSEPH'S CHARLEVILLE

# Chef Domini Kemp's Thai beef Salad

Serves: 4 as a light dish
Preparation time: 20 minutes, Cooking time: 10 minutes

**½ kg sirloin beef**
**1 tbsp olive oil**
**salt and freshly ground black pepper**

**Dressing**
**1 tbsp fish sauce**
**1 tbsp olive oil**
**1 tsp soft light brown sugar**
**2 cloves garlic, peeled and crushed**
**juice of two limes**
**1 tbsp sweet chilli sauce**

**Salad**
**1 red onion, peeled and sliced**
**1 cucumber, peeled and thinly sliced**
**1 pack cherry tomatoes, sliced in half**
**2 red chillis, deseeded and sliced**
**1 bunch spring onions, sliced**
**1 pack radishes, thinly sliced**
**50g coriander**
**1 bag mixed leaves**

Rub the beef with olive oil and season well before cooking on a very hot barbecue or pan for a few minutes on each side for medium rare. Remove from the heat and wrap in tin foil. Keep warm whilst you allow the beef to rest and prepare the other ingredients. Mix all the ingredients for the dressing and season with plenty of black pepper. Add all the salad ingredients to a large bowl and toss with the dressing. Slice the beef and mix with the salad and serve in a large bowl or individual plates.

DEDICATED TO: SMITH'S SUPERVALU, MONKSLAND, ATHLONE
NOMINATED LOCAL CHARITY: ST VINCENT DE PAUL

# Niamh Griffin's Zesty Meatballs

These meatballs are quick to make and taste delicious - they always go down well with my friends!

Serves: 4
Preparation time: 20 minutes
Cooking time: 25 - 35minutes

**500g lean mince meat**
**1 onion, finely chopped**
**2 cloves garlic, finely chopped**
**grated zest of one lemon**
**large bunch fresh basil, chopped**
**salt and pepper**
**1 tin chopped tomatoes or ½ large bottle passata**
**¼ tube tomato purée**
**1 glass red wine**
**olive oil (for cooking and finishing)**
**300g spaghetti**
**juice of half lemon**

Put the mince in a bowl and break up (to make it easy to mix).

Finely chop the onions and garlic and put in with the mince.

Add the finely grated lemon zest and the basil (keep aside some basil for the spaghetti later). Season with salt and pepper.

Mix all the ingredients together (using your hands is easiest) and then form approximately 16 meatballs from the mixture.

Heat a large frying pan with some olive oil in it until hot and add the meatballs. Brown the meatballs, turning so as to colour all over. This only takes a few minutes.

Once browned, add the tin of tomatoes or passata, some more salt and pepper, the tomato purée and glass of wine.

Allow to simmer for approximately 20 - 30 minutes until meatballs are cooked and sauce has reduced slightly.

When cooked, turn off the heat, but leave on the ring to keep warm. Cook the spaghetti and when cooked, drain immediately and drizzle some olive oil over it, squeeze the lemon juice in, and add the rest of the chopped basil with a little more salt and pepper.

Toss and put on the plate and divide the meatballs out with lots of sauce into the centre of the pasta on each plate.

For a spicy version you can add some finely chopped red chillis in with the meat mix.

DALY'S SUPERVALU, GREYSTONES
NOMINATED LOCAL CHARITY:
GREYSTONES CANCER SUPPORT

# Mary O'Rourke's Best Lasagne Ever

My friend's mom has been making this lasagne for years, and passed on the recipe to each of us when we first started having dinner parties. Never tasted one as nice!

Serves: 6
Preparation time: 30 minutes
Cooking time: 1½ hours

**Easi Cook lasagne sheets**
**For the Bolognese Sauce:**
1 tbsp olive oil
1 large onion, chopped
3 cloves garlic, crushed
400g round mince
1 tbsp mixed herbs
¾ 140g tube tomato puree
2 level tbsp tomato soup
1 400g tin tomatoes
100ml red wine
salt and pepper

**For the Cheese Sauce:**
3 tbsp butter
3 tbsp flour
1¼ pint milk
1 tsp English mustard
1 tsp ground nutmeg
200g cheddar cheese, grated
pepper

To make the Bolognese sauce, heat the oil in a pan, add the onions and garlic and sweat for approx 5-10 minutes until soft. Remove from the pan and leave to one side.

Put the mince into the pan on a high heat and stir until browned. Turn down the heat and add back in the onions and garlic.

Now add herbs, salt and pepper and tomato purée and stir in.

Sprinkle the two tablespoons of tomato soup over the mince and stir well. Add the wine and finally the tin of tomatoes.

Simmer over a medium heat for at least 1 hour. If the mince starts to look a little dry simply add in a little boiling water..

While this is cooking you can make the sauce. First make a roux by melting the butter in a pan, removing from the heat and adding the flour to make a thick paste. Then add the milk, a little at a time so that there are no lumps.

When all the milk is added, put back on the hob over a high heat and stir constantly until the sauce thickens and comes to the boil.

Turn the heat to the lowest setting and allow to simmer. While simmering, add the mustard, nutmeg and some freshly ground black pepper and stir. Next add the grated cheese, reserving a little for the top of the lasagne. When the cheese is melted the sauce is ready.

To assemble the lasagne, use a large lasagne dish; spread a layer of Bolognese sauce on the bottom, then a layer of cheese sauce, then a layer of lasagne sheets. Repeat this for a second layer. Then put one final layer of mince and sauce and sprinkle with the remaining cheese.

Cook in a preheated oven at 180°C for 25-30 minutes until bubbling and golden on top.

Delicious served with a fresh salad and some garlic bread!

BIRD'S SUPERVALU, NAVAN
NOMINATED LOCAL CHARITY: LOCAL MEALS ON WHEELS

# Martina Kilian's Guinness Stew

This is a typical welcoming dish for my many visitors, often after the 3 hour drive from Dublin airport – it's our 'Cead Mile Failte' stew!

Serves: 4 - 5
Preparation time: 20 - 30 minutes
Cooking time: 1 - 1½ hours

**1 kg prime Irish stewing beef**
**4 onions, chopped**
**500g carrots, chopped**
**1 can of Guinness**
**8-10 dried prunes or apricots**
**sunflower oil**
**salt and pepper**
**a few bay leaves**

Heat the oil until very hot then carefully add the beef. Season well.

Stir frequently to brown, then after a few minutes add the onions and mix well.

Allow to cook for a few minutes more, then add the carrots. Mix and pour the can of Guinness into the mix.

Cover with a lid and allow to simmer gently for 1 hour.

About 10 minutes before serving add the prunes or apricots and stir well.

Serve piping hot with potatoes.

SURLIS' SUPERVALU, TUBBERCURRY
NOMINATED LOCAL CHARITY: GALLAGHER HOUSE
RESOURCE CENTRE TUBBERCURRY

# Noreen O'Kelly's Oat and Apple Meat Balls

One day I experimented with oats and grated apple in my meatballs and it went down a treat! Everyone loved it, and it's been a family favourite ever since!

Serves: 6
Preparation time: 25 minutes
Cooking time: 30 minutes

**454g SuperValu mince**
**1 medium onion, chopped**
**1 medium apple, grated**
**250g Flahavan's Oatlets or similar**
**1 egg, beaten**
**good pinch of mixed herbs**
**1 packet oxtail or tomato Soup or**
**your own favourite pasta sauce**

Preheat the oven to 180°C

Mix the mince, onion, apple, oatlets and herbs in a large bowl.

Add the beaten egg and mix again.

Shape the mixture into balls and brown them lightly in a frying pan.

Transfer the meatballs into an ovenproof dish.

Make up the soup and pour this, or your own pasta sauce over the meatballs.

Cook in the oven for approx 30 minutes.

Serve with pasta.

SCALLY'S SUPERVALU, BLACKROCK
NOMINATED LOCAL CHARITY: CHERNOBYL GREATER CALL

# Mary Conway's Shepherd's Pie

This recipe is ideal for a large family like mine. It's filling, nutritious, and very tasty!

Serves: 7
Preparation time: 10 minutes
Cooking time: 30 minutes

**2 lb minced beef**
**1 large onion**
**6 mushrooms**
**1 carrot**
**4-6 large potatoes mashed**
**garden peas, corn or other vegetable of your choice**
**1 tbsp tomato sauce**
**Yorkshire relish**
**salt and pepper**

Dice all vegetables.

Fry onions and mushrooms and put to one side.

Fry mince, drain fat and season well. Add a few drops of Yorkshire relish.

Boil the vegetables until tender.

Add the vegetables, onion and mushroom to the meat and mix in the tomato sauce.

Put the mince mix into an oven proof dish, cover with mashed potato, and cook in a preheated oven (180°C) for approx 20 minutes to brown potatoes.

LYONS/DONLON SUPERVALU, TULLA
NOMINATED LOCAL CHARITY: CLARE CANCER SOCIETY

# Bernie Doyle's Creamy Spicy Beef

This was always my mothers 'Friday dinner' when we came in from school and I've carried on the tradition with my own kids.

Serves: 4
Preparation time: 10 minutes
Cooking time: 20 minutes

**1lb round beef steak**
**1 onion, finely chopped**
**1 cup mixed peppers, diced**
**3 tsp medium curry powder**
**1 tbsp mango chutney**
**1 tin of coconut milk**

Cut the steak into slivers and fry until tender (Approximately 5-8 minutes).

Add the onions and peppers and stir into meat.

Add the curry powder and cook for 30 seconds.

Add chutney and coconut milk and simmer for 10 minutes.

Adjust seasoning as required and serve with rice – delicious!

CROWE'S SUPERVALU, WEXFORD
NOMINATED LOCAL CHARITY: FRIENDS OF WEXFORD HOSPITAL

# Christina McCormack's Beef Curry

A good curry can be as mild or as hot as you like it. This is determined by your choice of curry powder – mild, medium or hot.

Serves: 4
Preparation time: 20 - 30 minutes
Cooking time: 20 minutes

**500g minced beef**
**1 onion, chopped**
**1 apple, chopped**
**100g raisins or sultanas**
**2 tsp tomato purée**
**2-3 tsp mango chutney**
**4 tomatoes or 1 tin of tomatoes**
**4-5 heaped tsp of curry powder**
**25g flour**
**a little cooking oil**
**salt and pepper**

Fry the onions and beef in oil until coloured, push to one side on pan and fry curry powder and flour in oil for 2 minutes.

Add tomato pureé, chutney and tomatoes and stir. Add water if necessary to make a sauce.

Add chopped apple and raisins or sultanas and stir well.

Cook gently in the pan for approximately 20 minutes until the meat is thoroughly cooked.

Season with salt and pepper, and serve with cooked rice.

MURPHY'S SUPERVALU, ROSSLARE HARBOUR
NOMINATED LOCAL CHARITY: RNLI ROSSLARE HARBOUR

# Anne Marie Dunne's Beef Roulade

Serves: 5
Preparation time: 20 minutes + 20 minutes refrigeration time
Cooking time: 40 minutes

**1 pack of ready made puff pastry**
**2 lb rib or round minced steak**
**1 bunch chives, chopped**
**1 bunch parsley, chopped**
**3 garlic cloves, crushed**
**½ onion, finely chopped**
**2 free range eggs**
**2 oz plain flour**
**1 tsp organic bouillon powder**
**½ tsp Herbamere seasoning**

Roll out puff pastry into a large square.

In a large bowl add the mince, chives, parsley, onion, garlic, bouillon powder, Herbamere seasoning, flour, and mix well.

Beat the eggs and add to the bowl, mix everything together well.

Spread the mix over the pastry until all the pastry is covered with the meat mix.

Now roll up like a Swiss roll.

Refrigerate roll for at least 20 minutes or until you are ready to use it.

Cut 5 slices 1-2 inches thick and place on a baking sheet lined with baking parchment.

Bake in a preheated oven at 200°C/400°F/Gas 6 for 35 - 40 minutes until pastry is fluffy and golden, and the mince is cooked.

Serve with seasonal vegetables.

Variation
This roulade can also be made with prime minced lamb and chopped fresh mint, or minced pork with grated cooking apple and apricots.

CREHAN/MCCABE'S SUPERVALU, CALLAN
NOMINATED LOCAL CHARITY: SPECIAL OLYMPICS

# Patricia Curtin's Lamb Shank Italian Style

Lamb shanks have recently become popular again. This is a lovely warming recipe on a cold day.

Serves: 4
Preparation time: 15 minutes
Cooking time: 2 hours

**4 lamb shanks**
**1 medium onion, chopped**
**1 medium carrot, sliced**
**1 stick celery, sliced**
**2 cloves garlic, crushed**
**1 tin chopped tomatoes**
**½ tsp thyme**
**½ tsp mixed herbs**
**1 tbsp sunflower oil**
**salt and pepper**

In a large heavy pot heat a tablespoon of sunflower oil and brown the meat.

Remove the meat, lower heat and fry the onions and garlic for 5 minutes.

Add the carrot and celery to the pan and fry for a few more minutes.

Add the chopped tomatoes and herbs.

Return the meat to the pot and simmer for 2 hours on a low heat.

Serve with rice or mashed potatoes.

HURLEY'S SUPERVALU, MIDLETON
NOMINATED LOCAL CHARITY: MIDLETON HOSPITAL

# Mary Martin's Spicy Lamb Kebabs with Sweet Chilli and Yoghurt Dip, and Herbed Couscous

I made this for our first barbecue this summer — it was fantastic!

Serves: 4
Preparation time: 20 minutes
Cooking time: 20 minutes

**1lb lamb, cubed**
**1 tsp cumin**
**1 tsp coriander seeds**
**½ tsp dried chilli flakes**
**2 cloves of garlic, crushed**
**2 tbsp olive oil**
**3 tbsp balsamic vinegar**
**freshly ground black pepper**
**1 red onion**
**1 red pepper**
**4-6 wooden skewers soaked in water**
  **for about 1 hour**
**250g Greek style yoghurt**
**1 tbsp sweet chilli sauce**
**couscous**
**chopped coriander and mint**
**garlic naan breads**

Toast the spices on a dry pan. Grind up the spices to make a marinade with the crushed garlic, balsamic vinegar and olive oil. Marinade the cubed lamb for at least an hour — this can also be done the night before.
Remove the core from the onion and cut into quarters.
Cut the red pepper into about 12 pieces.
Make up kebabs by skewering lamb pieces alternating with red onion and peppers. Depending on the length of your skewers you should have 4-6 kebabs. Grill these, cook on the barbecue or in a griddle pan turning occasionally.

Check lamb is cooked through by cutting into a chunk. Swirl the sweet chilli sauce into the yoghurt to make a dip for the kebabs. Prepare the couscous according to the packet and serve mixed with chopped coriander and mint. Griddle the naan breads and you will have a delicious summer dinner, perfect for your next barbecue!

KANE & MCCARTNEY'S SUPERVALU, RAHENY
NOMINATED LOCAL CHARITY:
ST FRANCIS HOSPICE, RAHENY

# Avril Humphries' Spicy Cornish Pasties

A mildly spicy version of an old favourite of ours.

Serves: 8 pasties
Preparation time: 10 minutes
Cooking time: 30 minutes

**450g lamb mince**
**1 tbsp vegetable oil**
**1 onion, finely chopped**
**2 tsp each coriander, turmeric and chilli powder**
**1 tsp each cumin and garam masala**
**450g petit pois**
**450g potatoes, diced and steamed**
**1 pack ready prepared shortcrust pastry sheets**
**salt and pepper**

Fry lamb mince in the oil for 4-5 minutes until browned. Then add onion and fry for a few inutes longer. Add all the spices to the pan and fry for 3 minutes.

Next add the peas, potatoes and a little seasoning, mix well and remove from the heat.

Unroll the pastry sheets and cut so that you have 8 equal sized pieces.

Spoon meat into the centre of each one and and fold over to shape into pasties, pressing the edges to seal.

Cook in a moderate oven preheated to 180°C for about 20 minutes or until the pastry is golden brown.

Serve on their own or with relish/gravy. Delicious!

TWOMEY'S SUPERVALU, DEANSGRANGE
NOMINATED LOCAL CHARITY: BARNARDO'S

# Annatina Quigley's Lamb Liver Deluxe

A quick meal for guests – the sauce can be done the evening before – delicious with side dishes

Serves: 4
Preparation time: 5 minutes
Cooking time: 30 minutes

**¼ onion**
**1 garlic clove (optional)**
**50g unsalted butter**
**1 tsp cornflour**
**glass of strong red wine e.g. shiraz**
**paprika (optional)**
**1-2 sprigs thyme or rosemary**
**1 cube beef stock, crumbled**
**600 - 700g lambs liver**
**salt and pepper**

Chop onion and garlic finely, and sauté gently in half the butter for 10-15 minutes until a rich, golden brown. Stir the cornflour through and then add red wine, paprika, thyme or rosemary, and leave to cook on a very gentle heat for 20-30 minutes unitl rich and thickened. Season to taste..

Cut the lambs liver in very thin slices, and fry in the remaining butter for 1-2 minutes each side.

Put it on a hot plate, pour a little water into the frying pan and scraping any sediment from the pan, add these juices to the sauce. Pour the sauce over the liver slices and serve.

REIDY'S SUPERVALU, MITCHELSTOWN
NOMINATED LOCAL CHARITY: TEARMONN UI CHAOIMH
DAY CARE CENTRE

# Nora Fisher's Pork Chops with Honey and Orange

A delicious and easy dish to prepare and cook.

Serves: 4
Preparation time: 10 minutes
Cooking time: 40 minutes

**4 pork chops**
**4 level tbsp clear honey**
**2 tbsp soy sauce**
**1 tbsp tomato ketchup**
**1 tbsp vinegar**
**1 tbsp tomato puree**
**salt and pepper**
**few drops Tabasco sauce**
**juice of 1 small orange**
**8 oz long grain rice**

Heat the oven to 375°F/190°C/Gas 5

Put the chops in a shallow cooking dish.

Blend all other ingredients except the rice and pour over the chops. Bake uncovered for 40 minutes, basting occasionally.

Cook rice as directed on pack. Drain rice and put into a serving dish and arrange chops on top.

Pour over any remaining sauce.

Serve with a green salad.

PETTITT'S SUPERVALU, ATHY
NOMINATED LOCAL CHARITY: ALZHEIMER'S
UNIT, ST VINCENT'S HOSPITAL, ATHY

# Sarah Kenny's BBQ Pork Chops with Mango Salsa

The salsa gives this dish a fresh summery feel. I like to serve this with sautéed potatoes or a baked potato.

Serves: 4
Preparation time: 20 minutes, plus 2 hours to marinade
Cooking time: 15 - 20 minutes

**4 pork chops**

**For the marinade:**
**50ml soy sauce**
**3 garlic cloves**
**thumb sized piece of ginger**
**1 tbsp lime juice**

**For the salsa:**
**1 large ripe mango**
**3 tbsp coriander**
**1 red chilli**
**1 small onion**
**1 tbsp lime juice**
**Pinch of sugar**

Mix the marinade ingredients in a blender.

Place the pork chops in a bowl or dish and pour the marinade over them. Refrigerate for 1-2 hours.

Dice mango, chop coriander, slice chilli and onion. Place these in a bowl with the other salsa ingredients. Stir and set aside.

Remove marinated pork chops from the fridge and grill or barbecue them until fully cooked.

Serve each chop accompanied by a generous serving of salsa, and potatoes cooked to your requirements.

COUGHLAN'S SUPERVALU, SHANKILL
NOMINATED LOCAL CHARITY: LOCAL ST VINCENT DE PAUL

# Cindy Soomoon Chin's Sweet and Sour Pork

This dish is an all-time favourite at our gatherings!

Serves: 6
Preparation time: 30 minutes
Cooking time: 25 minutes

**300g pork, cut into chunks**
**1 pepper, chopped**
**1 large onion, chopped**
**2 red chillies, finely chopped**
**¼ fresh pineapple, chopped**
**2 tomatoes, chopped**

**Pork Seasoning:**
**1 egg**
**1 tbsp light soy sauce**
**1 tbsp corn flour**

**Sauce:**
**3 tbsp tomato sauce**
**2 tbsp chilli sauce**
**2 tbsp plum sauce**
**1½ tbsp vinegar**
**3 tbsp sugar**
**200ml water**

Mix the pork with egg and soy sauce and leave for 10 - 15 minutes.

Then add the corn flour, dust off any excess and deep fry in hot oil for 5 - 10 minutes or until light golden brown. Remove from pan.

Make up the sauce by combining all the ingredients and mixing well.

Stir fry the peppers, onion, chilli, pineapple and tomatoes with oil in a wok. Add the sauce and mix well.

Finally, add the pork and stir for a few minutes more to combine all ingredients.

Serve on a bed of rice.

KENNY'S SUPERVALU, BLESSINGTON
NOMINATED LOCAL CHARITY: BLESSINGTON LIFE BOAT

# Siobhan Redahan's Fruity Pork and Peanut Kebabs

To me this is the taste of Saturday evenings in the summertime.

Serves: 4 -6
Preparation time: 20 minutes (plus 2 hours to marinate)
Cooking time: 15 - 20 minutes

**1½ lb pork loin, cut into chunks**
**2 tins of apricot halves, drained**
**2 green peppers cut into chunks**

**Marinade:**
**3 tbsp crunchy peanut butter**
**1 small onion, finely chopped**
**1 garlic clove crushed**
**1 tbsp brown sugar**
**1 tbsp lemon juice**
**1 tbsp soy sauce**
**4 tbsp olive oil**
**½ tsp chilli powder**
**1 tsp ground coriander**

Mix all marinade ingredients together in a big bowl.

Add pork, and leave to marinate for 2 hours.

Remove pork and thread onto skewers, alternating each chunk with a ½ apricot and a piece of green pepper.

Line a grill pan with foil and arrange kebabs on foil. Spoon over a little of the marinade.

Grill on a medium heat for 15-20 minutes, turning occasionally.

Serve with a green salad or lemon rice.

These are also delicious cooked on a barbecue!

GLANCY'S SUPERVALU, CARRICK-ON-SHANNON
NOMINATED LOCAL CHARITY: CONQUER CANCER

# Miriam Delahunty's Piglets in D Bags

When I was only small my Gran showed me how to make a magic meal in a bag!

Serves: 2
Preparation time: 10 minutes
Cooking time: 45 minutes

**1 tbsp Dijon mustard**
**2 pork chops**
**1 red pepper, chopped**
**2 small tomatoes, sliced**
**bunch of spring onions, chopped**
**4 rashers, cooked and chopped**
**3 peeled and sliced potatoes**
**salt and black pepper**

Spread the Dijon mustard on both sides of the chops and season with salt and pepper

Mix the peppers, tomatoes, spring onions and cooked rashers together and spoon the mixture onto the chops.

Place the sliced potatoes in a dish or a cooking bag. Carefully place the chops on top.

Cook at 180°C for about 45 minutes.

MCCONVILLE'S SUPERVALU, MONASTEREVIN
NOMINATED LOCAL CHARITY: MONASTEREVIN SPECIAL
OLYMPICS COMMITTEE

# Mary Prince's Creamy Pork with Mustard

This is something I put together a few years ago using just what was in the press. It's now a favourite in our house!

Serves: 6
Preparation time: 10 minutes
Cooking time: 25 minutes

**2 pork steaks, sliced finely**
**1 Spanish onion, chopped finely**
**200g button mushrooms, sliced**
**200g crème fraîche**
**½ chicken stock cube dissolved in 1 dsp hot water**
**4 tsp wholegrain mustard**
**1 glass of white wine**
**1 clove of garlic, crushed**
**A few strands of saffron in 1 tsp hot water**
**2 tsp olive oil**
**Salt and pepper**

Heat 1 teaspoon of olive oil in a pan.

Add the sliced pork steaks. Fry until the pork is nearly cooked (approximately 5 minutes). Remove and wrap in tin foil to keep warm.

Heat the other teaspoon of olive oil in the pan and add the onion and fry slowly (approximately 2 minutes).

Add the garlic and mushrooms and fry for a further 3 minutes.

Add the wine to the pan and allow to reduce for approx 5 minutes.

Add the remaining ingredients and simmer for 5 minutes.

Finally, add the pork back to the pan and continue to cook until the pork is cooked through (approximately 5 minutes).

Serve with rice.

RYAN'S SUPERVALU, GRANGE
NOMINATED LOCAL CHARITY: TIR NA N'ÓG RESPITE SERVICES

# Chef Aongus Hanly's
# Braised leg of lamb with tomato, chickpeas and chorizo

Spice up a traditional Leg of Lamb with this tasty tomato, chickpea and chorizo topping!

Serves: 4-6
Preparation time: 10 minutes
Cooking time: 2 hours - 2 hours 45 minutes

**1.5kg leg of lamb**
**150g chorizo, roughly chopped**
**1 tsp olive oil**
**1 glass of white wine**
**2 tins of chopped tomatoes**
**2 tins of chickpeas (drained)**
**salt and pepper**

Pre-heat the oven to 200°C.

Sprinkle the leg of lamb with salt and pepper. Place in a deep roasting tray. Put the lamb in the oven and seal it for 20 to 25 minutes or until it is nice and brown.

While the lamb is sealing sauté the chorizo with a little olive oil in a heavy bottomed sauce pan for 2-3 minutes, being careful not to scorch or burn it.

Add the white wine and let it evaporate almost to nothing. Add the chopped tomatoes and drained chickpeas. Season to taste. Warm the sauce thoroughly. When the lamb is sealed reduce the oven to 130°C.

Remove the lamb from the oven, pour the hot tomato sauce over the lamb. Cover the lamb and roasting tray with tin foil and secure it well.

Return to the oven. Continue to cook for 1 hour 30 minutes to 2 hours 15 minutes, depending on how well you like your lamb cooked. Remove from the oven, let rest for 10 minutes and serve.

DEDICATED TO: KAVANAGH'S SUPERVALU, CLAREMORRIS
NOMINATED LOCAL CHARITY: ST RITA'S

# Martine Lefevere's Very Special Tenderloin of Pork

This is my own invention; I love to experiment with food!

Serves: 4
Preparation time: 20 minutes
Cooking time: 20 minutes

**8 tbsp balsamic vinegar**
**1 tsp honey**
**1 tsp mustard**
**olive oil**
**4 level tsp sunflower seeds**
**1 red pepper, very finely chopped**
**1 green pepper, very finely chopped**
*few pinches of dried mixed herbs*
**mi instant noodles (or other thin noodle)**
**sunflower oil for deep frying**
**whites of 3 leeks, cut into extremely fine strips**
  **lengthwise**
**1 tbsp butter**
**12 pieces of tenderloin pork, each 3cm thick**
**2-3 tomatoes, washed and sliced into 12 slices**
**watercress**
**salt and pepper**

To make the sauce, whisk together the balsamic vinegar, honey and mustard.

Heat a splash of oil in a pan and fry the sunflower seeds for 2 minutes. Dry on kitchen paper. Mix with the peppers, mixed herbs, salt and pepper. Immerse the mi noodles in boiling water (needs only a few minutes to swell), then drain and keep warm.

Heat the sunflower oil in a deep pan; fry all the leek strips and dry on kitchen paper (use a skimmer to remove). They should be golden brown (not darker), curly and be crispy.

Heat the butter and sauté the meat for 3-4 minutes on each side. Season and keep warm in the oven with the plates.

Arrange 3 nests of fried leek around the middle of each plate, and place the meat in each one. Place a slice of tomato and a tablespoon of the pepper mix on top.

Arrange the noodles around the nests, drizzle with the sauce and serve with watercress.

WALSH'S SUPERVALU, CAHIRCIVEEN
NOMINATED LOCAL CHARITY: CAHIRCIVEEN HOSPICE

# Betty Denning's InyBorough Pork Loaf

A very simple recipe that has passed through 3 generations of the same family since the 1960s with a different twist each time

Serves: 4
Preparation time: 10 minutes
Cooking time: 1½ - 1 ¾ hours

**450g minced raw pork**
**450g minced raw ham**
**125g sausage meat**
**125g dried apricots, chopped**
**1 onion, finely chopped**
**1½ cups breadcrumbs**
**2 eggs unbeaten**
**¼ cup of milk**
**2 tbsp fresh parsley chopped**
**2 tbsp tomato ketchup**
**pepper**

Combine all the ingredients together very well – I use a Kenwood Chef to do this.

Spread the mixture into a large 2lb loaf tin and pack well down.

Bake in a pre-heated oven at 325°F/170°C/Gas 5 for 1½ - 1 ¾ hours depending on the depth of the tin.

When cooked remove from the oven and stand for 5 minutes.

Turn out on a flat plate and spread very lightly with a little honey. Return to the oven for 10 minutes – this gives the finished loaf a lovely glaze.

This can be served hot or cold. If serving cold it's delicious with a herby salad coated in a good extra virgin olive oil, and also some Cherry Tomatoes and white cheddar cheese.

HARRIS' SUPERVALU, BAILEBOROUGH
NOMINATED LOCAL CHARITY: BAILEBOROUGH CANCER FUND

# John Handly's Daddy's Sauce

My Dad used to make this. It's a real taste of home. Use it as a marinade rather than a condiment.

Preparation time: 20 minutes

**½ glass of red wine**
**3 chillis, deseeded (optional) and roughly chopped**
**2 tsp Worcestershire sauce**
**3 onions, roughly chopped**
**2 tsp soy sauce**
**2 cloves garlic, roughly chopped**
**sea salt**
**ground black pepper**

Liquidise all the ingredients with a little seasoning.

Pour over ribs, or your preferred meat and allow to marinate.

Cook on the barbecue for maximum taste.

CASEY'S SUPERVALU, LUSK
NOMINATED LOCAL CHARITY: OUR LADY'S HOSPITAL, CRUMLIN

# Poultry
Recipes

# Clodagh McKenna's Provence Chicken Casserole

I ate a dish similar to this last autumn in France. Using a good Irish chicken and local herbs this is so good to come home to during the colder months.

Serves: 4
Preparation time: 10 minutes
Cooking time: 1 hour 40 minutes

**olive oil**
**1 whole organic or free range chicken,**
  **jointed into 8 pieces**
**4 cloves of garlic, peeled**
**salt and pepper**
**4 tbsp of dry white wine**
**bunch of fresh tarragon**
**leaves from 1 sprig of rosemary**
**leaves from 1 sprig of thyme**
**350ml chicken stock**

Place a casserole dish over a medium heat and add in a dollop of olive oil. When the oil is hot add in the chicken pieces and lightly brown all over for 4-5 minutes. Then add in the garlic, season with salt and pepper and allow to cook for a further minute.

Pour the wine over chicken, followed by the stock and bring to the boil. Roughly chop up all the fresh herbs and add to the casserole, stir and cover.

Place in a pre-heated oven at 140°C for 1½ hours.

Tip
Delicious served with Gratin Dauphinois potatoes (see p143)

DEDICATED TO: MURPHY'S SUPERVALU, LEIXLIP
NOMINATED LOCAL CHARITY: IRISH HEART FOUNDATION

# Maria Hughes' Melo's Wings

I love chicken wings when eating out but they are never the same when you buy them frozen, so I decided to start making my own. They're now a favourite at our parties of both young and old!

Serves: 4
Preparation time: 10 minutes
Cooking time: 20 - 25 minutes

**16 fresh chicken wings**
**sprinkle of ground ginger**
**2 tbsp light soy sauce**
**1 tbsp dark soya sauce**
**2 tbsp sweet chilli sauce (or to taste)**
**Sea salt to season**

Preheat oven to 200°C/400°F/Gas 6 or the barbecue to medium-high.

Snip and discard the wing tips and separate wings into two pieces.

Place the wings in a large bowl and season with ground ginger.

Add the light and dark soy sauces, and the sweet chilli sauce.

Stir mixture well ensuring all the wings are coated. Season with salt.

Cook for 20-25 minutes in the oven or on the barbecue.

Enjoy!

MURPHY'S SUPERVALU, BALLYMUN
NOMINATED LOCAL CHARITY: ST FRANCIS HOSPITAL RAHENY

# Zoe Armstrong's Spatchcock Tandoori Chicken

A delicious and succulent, spicy roast chicken dish.

Serves: 4
Preparation time: 15 minutes
Cooking time: 1¼ -1½ hours

**1 whole chicken (about 1.5kg)**
**1 tub of fat free fromage frais**
**3 cloves garlic, crushed**
**1 thumb size piece of ginger, grated**
**1 or 2 little hot chillies (according to your taste), chopped**
**zest and juice of one lime**
**1 tbsp olive oil**
**2 tsp each; cayenne pepper, curry powder, ground cumin, ground coriander**
**salt and pepper to season**

To spatchcock your chicken, place it breast side down on a chopping board and using a good kitchen scissors, cut out the spine. Turn the chicken over and squash down on the breastbone (to break it) using the flat of your palm.
Mix all the remaining ingredients (except the oil) together and season well. Make a pocket between the chicken skin and the breast and leg meat using your hand. Spoon and spread the tandoori mixture into this pocket.
Place the chicken, breast side up, into a roasting tin and brush the skin with a little olive oil and season (At this stage if you wish you can put the chicken into the fridge until you're ready, the flavours will only improve).
Roast for about 1¼ to 1½ hours. Baste 2-3 times during the cooking time.
This is perfect served with a green salad. I like it with a tomato and green bean salad.  It's delicious, try it!

COLLINS' SUPERVALU, CARRIGALINE
NOMINATED LOCAL CHARITY: MARYMOUNT HOSPICE

# Judith Coffey's Chicken with Mushrooms & Mustard sauce

My father used to make a delicious Steak Diane Sauce. Although this recipe varies worldwide, I remember some of his main ingredients and have recreated my own version for chicken.

Serves: 2
Preparation time: 15 minutes
Cooking time: 15 minutes

**2 chicken breasts**
**olive oil - a little to cook**
**1 onion, finely chopped**
**6 mushrooms, finely chopped**
**3-4 garlic cloves, crushed**
**salt and pepper**
**several dashes of Worcestershire sauce**
**a few drops of milk (optional)**
**½ carton crème fraîche**
**1 dsp Dijon mustard (more if preferred)**
**1 tsp brown sugar**

Place chicken breasts on heated pan with a little olive oil.

Add chopped onion, mushrooms, crushed garlic, seasoning, a few dashes of Worcestershire sauce and cook on low heat so as to sauté the onion and mushrooms.

If it is a little dry add a few drops of milk to keep creamy. Turn chicken, as you don't want it to brown.

Add the mustard, sugar and a few more dashes of Worcestershire sauce.

GARVEY'S SUPERVALU, COBH
NOMINATED LOCAL CHARITY: COBH COMMUNITY CENTRE

At this stage the chicken, mushroom and onions should be cooked but as it's done on a low heat, the chicken absorbs the garlic flavour.

Then add the ½ carton of crème fraîche. Turn the chicken in it and lightly mix into the mushroom/onion/mustard sauce mix. You now have the chicken breasts in a delicious creamy sauce that was simple to make!

I like to serve this chicken dish with new potatoes tossed in butter and fresh parsley, also mange tout! These can be prepared whilst the chicken is cooking.

Also, serve a basket of french bread on the side. (Oh, and of course, a nice glass of Sauvignon Blanc!)

# Vera Chambers's Chicken and Apple Casserole

My family love this dish, as do I because it's quick and easy to prepare and inexpensive.

Serves: 4
Preparation time: 10 minutes
Cooking time: 1 hour 5 - 1 hour 10 minutes

**2 tbsp oil**
**4 chicken portions, skin removed**
**2 onions, chopped**
**4 streaky rashers, chopped**
**2 crisp dessert apples, peeled, cored and thickly sliced**
**2 level tbsp plain flour**
**½ pint cider**
**¼ pint chicken stock or water**
**salt and pepper**

Preheat oven to 200°C/400°F/Gas 6.

Heat the oil in a deep pan. Season the chicken and brown all over for 6 or 7 minutes. Remove and place in a casserole dish.

In the same pan, fry the onion and bacon for approximately 5 minutes and then add both to the casserole dish.

Sauté the apple for 1-2 minutes each side until golden, and add to the casserole dish also. Now, mix the flour, and stock/water in the pan until dissolved, and bring to the boil, stirring.

Add this mixture to the casserole dish, stir, cover and cook in the centre of the oven for 45-50 minutes, until the chicken is cooked through and the sauce thickened.

CAULFIELD'S SUPERVALU, BANDON
NOMINATED LOCAL CHARITY: HYPERBARIC CHAMBER FUND

# James Ryan's Duck and Pineapple

I tried this dish just to see how it worked, and to impress the girlfriend!

Serves: 4
Preparation time: 20 minutes
Cooking time: 1 hour

**1 tbsp olive oil**
**4 x 225g duck fillets**
**4 slices of fresh pineapple, cut into fingers**
**(approximately 1cm thick and including the core)**
**2 tbsp sweet chilli sauce**
**1 onion, sliced**
**salt and pepper**

Remove and reserve the skin from the duck fillets. Heat 1 tablespoon of the oil in a pan and fry the duck fillets for 2-3 minutes each side to seal well.

Meanwhile layer the pineapple pieces onto the base of a roasting dish. Remove the duck from the pan and place on top of the pineapple. Drizzle with the remaining tablespoon olive oil and sprinkle with salt and pepper. Roast in a preheated oven (190°C) for 12-15 minutes until just pink in the centre.

Meanwhile, to make a sauce, fry small bits the reserved of duck fat with sweet chilli sauce and some salt for 2-3 minutes. Remove all the solid fat from the pan and add onions. Sauté for 4-5 minutes until softened, and just catching colour. Spoon this mixture over the cooked duck, and serve with baked potatoes or rice.

BARRY DOWN'S SUPERVALU, BALLINCOLLIG
NOMINATED LOCAL CHARITY: BROTHERS OF CHARITY

# Nora McGuire's Grape Filled Chicken

I tried something similar to this dish in a hotel 25 years ago. This is my own version of the delicious recipe.

Serves: 1
Preparation time: 5 minutes
Cooking time: 45 minutes

**1 chicken fillet**
**2 tsp of soft, rindless goats cheese**
**4 or 5 green or red grapes, sliced in half**
**5 tbsp Bulmers Light cider**
**tarragon**
**salt and pepper**

Slice the chicken fillet to make a pocket.

Spread the cheese inside this pocket and fill with grapes.

Season the chicken with tarragon, salt and pepper.

Place the chicken in an ovenproof dish and pour the Bulmers Light cider over it.

Leave uncovered and bake in a pre-heated oven at 200°C/400°F/Gas 5 for approx 45 minutes.

Make sure to spoon the juices over the chicken at regular intervals while cooking

To serve 4 people simply multiply all ingredients by 4.

# Mary Gould's Chicken Stuffed with Bacon

A real Irish twist on this simple traditional dinner.

Serves: 4
Preparation time: 10 minutes
Cooking time: 20 - 25 minutes

**4 chicken fillets**
**8 slices Clonakilty black pudding**
**4 streaky rashers (or 8 depending on size of chicken breast)**
**1 bag of SuperValu baby potatoes**
**2-3 knobs of butter**
**bunch of parsley**

Make a pocket in the chicken fillets.

Stuff the pocket with the black pudding.

Wrap the rasher around the chicken breast, tuck the ends underneath the breast and place on a baking tray.

Cook in a preheated oven 375°F/190°C/Gas 5 for approx 25 minutes. Ensure these are cooked through before serving.

Serve with the baby potatoes mixed with parsley and melted butter.

MOLONEY'S SUPERVALU, BALLINA
NOMINATED LOCAL CHARITY: THE AISLING GROUP

RYAN'S SUPERVALU, KILMALLOCK
NOMINATED LOCAL CHARITY: TIR NA N'ÓG RESPITE SERVICES

# Kevin McCann's Chicken Carruth

There were many things that led to the creation of this recipe; including learning to cook, my German mother-in-law's gorgeous meatloaf and Michael Carruth winning a gold medal at the Barcelona Olympics.

Serves: 4
Preparation time: 20 minutes
Cooking time: 40 minutes

**2 tbsp oil**
**4 chicken breasts**
**1 tbsp paprika**
**1 tbsp turmeric**
**4 smoked rashers**
**1 medium onion, diced**
**2 cloves garlic, crushed**
**1 tsp mixed herbs**
**1 chicken stock cube**
**2 tbsp mango chutney**
**1 tbsp tomato puree**
**1 tsp mustard**
**1 tbsp lemon juice**
**100ml cream**
**Salt and pepper to taste**
**Sprig of parsley**

Cut chicken into 1cm (½") strips; coat with paprika and turmeric and leave to sit for at least 20 minutes.

Heat oil in a large pot. Cut the rashers into small pieces and fry well in pot. Add onions, garlic and mixed herbs to the rashers and gently fry until the onions are soft.

Put broken up stock cube, mango chutney, tomato purée and mustard in ½ pint boiling water; stir well and add to pot. Simmer for 15 minutes.

Pan fry the chicken in a little oil until cooked through and browned on the outside; add to pot.

Put in half the lemon juice, salt and pepper; stir well. Taste and adjust as required. Cook gently for another 5 minutes.

Add cream just before serving and garnish with the parsley.

Serve with basmati rice and broccoli, cooked al dente with a hint of nutmeg.

FLEMING'S SUPERVALU, MONAGHAN
NOMINATED LOCAL CHARITY: MONAGHAN BRANCH,
SPECIAL OLYMPICS

# Sheila Nolan's Creamy Chicken Bake

This is a quick and easy dish to make, but is really tasty!
It's ideal for fussy eaters because you can tailor it by adding
whatever vegetable they like.

Serves: 6
Preparation time: 20 minutes
Cooking time: 45-50 minutes

**6 chicken fillets, sliced**
**150g mushrooms, sliced**
**¼ red pepper, sliced**
**¼ green pepper, sliced**
**2 large onions, chopped**
**10 cherry tomatoes, sliced**
**a few fresh basil leaves**
**salt and pepper**
**500ml cream**
**100g breadcrumbs**
**150g grated cheese**

Take 6 individual ceramic pie dishes and cover the bottoms with
a row of chicken slices (equalling one breast per dish). Cover
with the vegetables and cherry tomatoes. Season as you go.

Add a few basil leaves to each dish.

Pour over the cream and then sprinkle some breadcrumbs on
each dish, then top with cheese.

Bake in a preheated oven at 180°C for approximately 30
minutes until chicken is cooked.

Serve with baby new potatoes and petit pois.

QUISH'S SUPERVALU, TRAMORE
NOMINATED LOCAL CHARITY: MEALS ON WHEELS,
TRAMORE

# Fergal O'Malley's Crispy Potato Jackets with Bacon and Chicken

These make a delicious snack, or serve with a side salad and chips for a tasty dinner

Serves: 4
Preparation time: 15 minutes
Cooking time: 50-55 minutes

**4 large baking potatoes**
**½ lb back bacon**
**1 tbsp olive oil**
**2 cooked chicken breasts, diced**
**100g cheddar cheese**
**4 tbsp sweet chilli sauce**
**salt and black pepper**

Cut the potatoes in half and scoop out the centre. (Use the potato part for mash, or in a soup or stew)

Bake the shells in a preheated oven at 350° F/ 180° C/ Gas 4 for 45-50 minutes until cooked and crispy.

Meanwhile, cut the bacon into strips.

Heat olive oil in a pan and fry the bacon for 3-4 minutes until crispy. Add chicken, sweet chilli sauce and seasoning and allow to gently warm through for 3-4 minutes.

When the potato skins are crispy, remove from the oven and fill with the bacon and chicken. Cover with grated cheese.

Place under a hot grill until the cheese melts.

CAROLAN'S SUPERVALU, KINGSCOURT
NOMINATED LOCAL CHARITY: CAVAN HOSPICE

# Winnie Ubutlibut's Chicken and Basil

A simple Thai recipe without the hassle.

Serves: 2
Preparation time: 3 minutes
Cooking time: 10 minutes

**2 chicken breast fillets, cubed**
**1 clove of garlic, chopped finely (optional)**
**1 small onion, chopped**
**2 tbsp cooking oil**
**1 tbsp fish sauce or oyster sauce**
**a handful of fresh basil leaves**

Sauté the garlic and onion gently.

Add in the chicken and stir fry for 5 minutes.

Add the fish sauce or oyster sauce to the pan and stir. Allow chicken to cook through.

Lastly, add the fresh basil and stir again.

Remove from the heat and serve immediately with rice.

GARVEY'S SUPERVALU, DINGLE
NOMINATED LOCAL CHARITY: THE AISLING GROUP

# Bronagh Maguire's Bombay Butter Bean Pasta

My sister came up with this sauce because she was bored with Bolognese. My kids always come back for more!

Serves: 6
Preparation time: 15 minutes
Cooking time: 35 minutes

**1 tbsp olive oil**
**1 large onion chopped**
**3 garlic cloves finely chopped**
**1 tin chopped tomatoes**
**½ jar Bunalin Crushed Tomatoes**
**1 tin butter beans**
**6 chicken fillets cubed**
**1 heaped tbsp Garam Masala**
**1 tsp chilli powder**
**1 tsp ground coriander**
**1 tsp ground cumin**
**1 tub crème fraîche**
**2 tbsp chopped fresh coriander**
**Salt and pepper**

Heat oil in a large pan and gently soften chopped onions and garlic. Add the chicken cubes and cook for 5 minutes
Add the powdered and ground spices and some salt and pepper
Allow to coat the chicken, onions and garlic in the pan
Add chopped and crushed tomatoes and simmer for 10 – 15 minutes
Drain the butter beans and add to the pan. Simmer for a further 10-15 minutes until chicken is cooked through
Add crème fraîche and chopped coriander just before serving
Serve on a bed of tagliatelle

BYRNE'S SUPERVALU, HACKETSTOWN
NOMINATED LOCAL CHARITY: ST JOHNS DAYCARE CENTRE

# Beryl Teape's Chicken Clonatore

A perfect chicken dish for a romantic dinner for two!

Serves: 2
Preparation time: 20 minutes
Cooking time: 30 minutes

**2 free range chicken breasts, cut into pieces**
**1 onion, peeled and chopped**
**3 garlic cloves, peeled and chopped**
**1 courgette**
**6 breakfast mushrooms**
**3 peppers (1 green, 1 yellow, 1 red)**
**2 cans plum tomatoes**
**3 tbsp olive oil**
**4 fl oz red wine**
**2 tsp sugar**
**2 tbsp tomato puree**
**8 fresh basil leaves**
**3 tbsp freshly whipped cream**
**salt and pepper**

In a large deep frying pan brown the chicken pieces in olive oil for approximately 5-10 minutes.

Remove from the pan and place to one side.

Add garlic to the pan and cook gently for a minute.

Add wine and cook until mixture boils and reduces by half.

Puree together the plum tomatoes, tomato puree, basil and onion and add to the pan.

Add sugar and seasoning and bring to the boil.

Stir in mushrooms, courgette, peppers and cook for approximately 15 minutes.

Add the chicken and cook for another 15 minutes (or until chicken is cooked through).

Add the cream and mix through.

Serve immediately with potatoes roasted with rosemary.

SCALLY'S SUPERVALU, CLONAKILTY
NOMINATED LOCAL CHARITY: COPE FOUNDATION

84

# Marie Simpson's Chicken with Goats Cheese and Watercress in a Honey Mustard dressing

A tasty dinner party dish which can be made well in advance. Once in the oven it needs little attention and it never fails to impress!

Serves: 4
Preparation time: 15 minutes
Cooking time: 30 minutes

**4 large chicken breasts**
**200g rindless goats cheese**
**50g watercress, roughly chopped**
**1 tbsp olive oil**
**4 tbsp wholegrain mustard**
**2 tbsp runny honey**

Cut a pocket into each of the chicken breasts.

In a bowl mash together the goats cheese and chopped watercress. Stuff this mixture into the cut pockets of the chicken breast.

Place the stuffed chicken in an ovenproof dish and preheat the oven to 180°C.

Mix the oil, mustard and honey to make a dressing. Pour over the chicken breasts.

Cook in the oven for approximately 30 minutes or until the chicken is cooked through, spooning the juices over the chicken at intervals.

O'TOOLE'S SUPERVALU, TUAM
NOMINATED LOCAL CHARITY: TUAM CANCER CARE

# Claire Brett-Holmes' Chicken & Vegetable Tagliatelle

I came up with this recipe by combining my own favourite tastes and it's a real winner with the whole family.

Serves: 4
Preparation time: 15 minutes
Cooking time: 15 minutes

**4 chicken breasts**
**1 onion**
**1 clove garlic**
**1 each red, yellow and green pepper**
**1 courgette, sliced**
**6-8 mushrooms, sliced**
**few sprigs fresh parsley**
**jar of Sacla Tomato and Parmesan sauce (or other good quality sauce)**
**½ tin of chopped tomatoes**
**3 tbsp cream**
**pack tagliatelle pasta**

Cut the chicken into bite size pieces and sauté in a pan. Transfer to a saucepan.

Finely chop the onion and garlic, and sauté lightly.

Add sliced peppers, then courgette and gently sauté.

Combine with the chicken and add jar of sauce and chopped tomatoes.

Allow to simmer under gentle heat for 10-15 minutes.

Meanwhile cook pasta (8-10 minutes) in boiling water with a drop of olive oil.

Just before serving add the cream to the main dish.

Drain pasta.

Serve with main dish over pasta, garnished with a sprig of parsley.

MORIARTY'S SUPERVALU, SKERRIES
NOMINATED LOCAL CHARITY: LOCAL MEALS ON WHEELS

# Sean Kearney's Spicy Chicken Pasta

A blend of mild curry cooked with chicken and pasta in a special recipe sauce.

Serves: 4
Preparation time: 15 minutes
Cooking time: 10 minutes

**olive oil**
**4 chicken breasts, cubed**
**1-2 cloves of garlic**
**1-2 chillies, finely chopped**

**250ml fresh cream**
**2 tbsp mild curry powder**
**4 portion of penne pasta**
**handful of basil**

Heat olive oil in a wok. Brown chicken, then add garlic and chillies.

Add cream and curry powder, stir well.

While chicken is cooking in the wok, cook pasta in a separate pot.

Chop basil and add to the wok, stir for about 5 minutes - check chicken is cooked through.

Place pasta in a bowl and pour chicken and sauce generously over it.

Delicious served with naan bread.

MORIARTY'S SUPERVALU, PALMERSTOWN
NOMINATED LOCAL CHARITY: LOCAL MEALS ON WHEELS

# Bob White's Chicken Curry in a Wok

I made this dish up myself and have been using it regularly for a few years, sometimes using prawns instead of chicken.

Serves: 6
Preparation time: 10 minutes
Cooking time: 25 minutes

**6 chicken breasts, cubed**
**2 tsp of turmeric**
**2 tsp chilli powder (or to your taste)**
**2 tsp coriander**
**1 tsp ground ginger**
**1 tsp cumin**
**6 cloves of garlic chopped**
**8 oz (225g) mushrooms, quartered**
**2 medium onions, chopped**
**1 tin coconut milk**
**1 tin chopped tomatoes**
**225ml chicken stock (using 2 stock cubes)**

Mix all the spices together in a cup.

Sweat onions and garlic and put aside.

Brown chicken in the wok and put aside.

Heat a little olive oil and fry spices for a minute or two, then add enough stock to make a paste.

Add the remaining stock and all ingredients.

Simmer for approximately 20 minutes or until the chicken is cooked through. Serve over rice

SMITH'S SUPERVALU, KINSALE
NOMINATED LOCAL CHARITY: KINSALE HOSPITAL

# Joan Finlay's Thai Green Curry

This is my favourite recipe and it's ideal for 'casual dining'. Don't be put off by the long list of ingredients it is worth the effort!

Serves: 4
Preparation time: 20 minutes
Cooking time: 20 minutes

**For the Green Curry Paste:**
**50g coriander (leaves only but keep stalks for the curry)**
**5 green chillies or to taste**
**3 stalks lemongrass**
**4 shallots**
**3 cloves garlic**
**3cm ginger**
**25g basil**
**5 strips lime peel**
**2 tbsp olive oil**
**salt and pepper**

**For the Curry**
**1 tbsp olive oil**
**6-8 shallots halved (or really small onions quartered)**
**2 cloves garlic chopped**
**300ml chicken stock (cubes naturally!)**
**3-4 tbsp thai fish sauce (nam pla)**
**½ tsp brown sugar**
**3 strips lime peel**
**100g French beans**
**chicken fillets (allow one per person) cut into strips**
**2 tins coconut milk**
**juice of 1 lime**

For the paste, place all the ingredients in a food processor and process to paste. Leave herbs until the end. This can be made in advance and stored in a sealed jar in the fridge.

Heat oil in a large pan, add shallots (or onions); cook until golden brown. Add 2 tablespoons of the paste and fry for 2 minutes. Add stock, 2 tablespoons fish sauce, brown sugar, lime peel; cook for 2-3 minutes.
Add chicken and cook for further 6-8 minutes or until cooked thoroughly. Add the beans and the stalks from the coriander along with the coconut milk and heat through. Add the remainder of the paste (important to retain bright green colour) and adjust the flavour with extra fish sauce if necessary, add juice of lime.

Serve with boiled rice.

DELANEY'S SUPERVALU. RATHDOWNEY
NOMINATED LOCAL CHARITY: THE AISLING GROUP

# Sujittra Rupsantat's Thai Red Curry

This is a recipe my mum taught me. It's one of my favourite dishes.

Serves: 4-6
Preparation time: 15 minutes
Cooking time: 25 minutes

**2 tins coconut milk**
**2 tbsp red curry paste**
**4 chicken breasts, sliced**
**2 courgettes, diced**
**2 green peppers, diced**
**2 red peppers, diced**
**1 red chilli, deseeded (optional), finely sliced**
**2 tbsp fish sauce**
**2 tsp sugar**

Over a moderate heat combine the coconut milk and red curry paste in a large pot, bringing slowly to a simmer.

Add the chicken and simmer for 2-3 minutes.

Add the courgettes, peppers and chilli, and then add the fish sauce and simmer for 3 minutes.

Add the sugar, and simmer for 15 minutes or until the chicken is cooked through.

Serve with rice.

SUPERVALU, BALALLY, SANDFORD
NOMINATED LOCAL CHARITY: CRUMLIN CHILDREN'S
HOSPITAL

# Rozina Giul's Chicken Pilao

A delicious rice dish which is sure to get your mouth watering!

Serves: 6-8
Preparation time: 10 minutes + 15 minutes soaking time
Cooking time: 15-20 minutes + 5-10 minutes standing time

**6 chicken legs**
**1kg basmati rice**
**2 onions, chopped**
**3 cloves garlic, chopped**
**1 tsp chopped ginger**
**2 large tomatoes, chopped**
**5 tbsp olive oil**
**3 tsp cumin**
**salt and pepper to season**

Rinse rice in cold water and leave to sit in a bowl of water for 15 minutes. Drain and cook in salted water according to pack instructions.

Meanwhile, heat the oil and fry the onions until brown.

Add the tomatoes, garlic and ginger and allow to cook for approximately 5 minutes, stirring occasionally.

Add the chicken, salt, pepper and cumin. Stir fry for about 10 minutes, adding a little water if needed.

Add the cooked rice to the frying pan and mix together with the chicken and other ingredients.

Remove from the heat and cover the pan with a clean wet kitchen cloth. Leave for 5-10 minutes and then serve.

Delicious served with plain yoghurt mixed with mint, salt and chopped cucumber.

O'KEEFFE'S SUPERVALU, MILLSTREET
NOMINATED LOCAL CHARITY: THE DAY CARE CENTRE
MILLSTREET

# Ciara Butler's Lime and Ginger Chicken Ciabatta

I was making a steak sandwich and ran out of steak, so I marinated some chicken, added pesto and mozzarella. The result was fantastic!

Serves: 2
Preparation time: 10 minutes, (plus 10 minutes marinating time)
Cooking time: 15 minutes

**juice of 1 lime**
**½ inch root ginger, grated**
**2 chicken fillets**
**sea salt and freshly ground black pepper**
**½ red onion, chopped**
**6 cherry tomatoes**
**ciabatta bread**
**olive oil**
**mayonnaise**
**4 lettuce leaves**
**mozzarella cheese**
**Pine nuts**
**Sundried tomato pesto or tomato relish**

Add the juice of the lime and the grated ginger to the chicken fillets.

Sprinkle with sea salt and freshly ground black pepper. Leave to marinate for 10 minutes.

Roughly chop the red onion, slice the tomatoes and wash lettuce leaves. Slice mozzarella into thin slices.

Heat the ciabatta bread until warm and golden in colour. Slice lengthwise.

Place sliced tomatoes under a hot grill until soft, drizzling with olive oil before cooking.

Cook the marinated chicken breasts on a grill pan for 10 minutes until nicely charred and cooked through.

Assemble by spreading mayonnaise on the base of the ciabatta. Place two leaves of lettuce on this followed by a chicken breast.

Carefully place the grilled tomatoes on the chicken and add the red onion.

Layer the mozzarella on top, sprinkle some pine nuts over the cheese and add a generous dash of sun dried tomato pesto or tomato relish.

Place under a grill until the cheese melts.

CAULFIELD'S SUPERVALU, TIPPERARY
NOMINATED LOCAL CHARITY: TIPPERARY SOUTH HOSPICE

# Sheila Doyle's Garden Chicken

This is a very tasty chicken dish. You just can't beat the flavour and fragrance of freshly picked garden herbs.

Serves: 4
Preparation time: 15 minutes
Cooking time: 20 minutes

**1 large fennel bulb**
**4 chicken breasts**
**100ml single cream**
**1 tbsp olive oil**
**3 garlic cloves, finely chopped**
**handful of garden herbs e.g. thyme, parsley, tarragon**

Dice the fennel.

Heat the olive oil in a pan and add the finely chopped garlic and diced fennel.

Cook for 5 – 10 minutes until fennel is soft and sweet smelling.

Dice the chicken and add to the pan.

Fry for a further 10 minutes until chicken is cooked.

Stir in the cream and finely chopped herbs.

Serve with rice.

PETTITT'S SUPERVALU, GOREY
NOMINATED LOCAL CHARITY: ST AIDAN'S DAY CARE
CENTRE, GOREY

# Clodagh McKenna's Pitta with Grilled Lemon Chicken and Greek Yoghurt

This is scrumptious anytime of the day! The chicken and vegetables can also be grilled on a bbq so perfect for the summer time too.

Serves: 4
Preparation time: 10 minutes (plus 30 minutes marinating)
Cooking time: 10 minutes

**4 chicken breasts (free range or organic, skinned)**
**juice of 1 lemon**
**1 tbsp olive oil**
**100g greek yoghurt**
**1 roasted red pepper (sliced)**
**2 spring onions (thinly sliced)**
**4 pitta breads**
**lettuce**
**salt and pepper**
**few sprigs of fresh coriander**

Marinate the chicken breasts in the lemon juice for half an hour in the fridge and then pan grill the chicken in the oil for 5 minutes on each side.

When the chicken is cooked slice up into small pieces and place in a bowl. Add in the greek yoghurt, sliced roasted red pepper and spring onions, season with salt and pepper and mix well.

Grill or toast the pitta bread, slice down the side and prise open.

Stuff the pitta with some salad leaves, coriander and the lemon, yoghurt and chicken salad. YUM!

DEDICATED TO: SINGLETON'S SUPERVALU, HOLLYHILL
NOMINATED LOCAL CHARITY: ST MARY'S ON THE HILL

# Norah Sheahan's Cream Chicken

This tasty, yet simple creamy chicken dish is my own invention

Serves: 4
Preparation time: 15 minutes
Cooking time: 40-45 minutes

**4 chicken fillets**
**4 oz white flour**
**1 tbsp olive oil**
**1 onion, chopped**
**4 smoked rashers, chopped**
**250g mushrooms, quartered**
**600ml chicken stock**
**2 oz butter**
**1 glass white wine**
**½ pint cream**
**salt and pepper**

Cut the chicken into bite size pieces, toss with half the flour, and season with salt and pepper
Heat a little oil in a pan and brown the chicken for a few minutes. Turn down the heat a little and add the onions, rashers and mushrooms, allowing the onions to soften for a few minutes. Tip everything into a casserole dish with enough chicken stock to cover. Season. Bake in a preheated oven at 180°C for 30 minutes (until cooked through)
When cooked, remove from the oven. Make a roux by melting the butter and mixing in the remaining 2oz of flour. Add to the chicken a teaspoon at a time, finally adding the wine and cream. Simmer for 5-6 minutes until thickened. If you like, you can chop some pineapple in at this stage as an extra twist
Serve with mashed potatoes or rice and a green salad to mop up the juices

GARVEY'S SUPERVALU, LISTOWEL
NOMINATED LOCAL CHARITY: LISTOWEL HOSPICE

# Fish
Recipes

# Clodagh McKenna's Spicy Fish Cakes

Serves: 4
Preparation time: 20 minutes (plus 30 minutes chilling time)
Cooking time: 20 minutes

**25g butter**
**55g onion, finely chopped**
**2 chillies de-seeded and chopped**
**55g mashed potato**
**115g cooked cod or haddock**
**1 egg yolk**
**1 tablespoon of chopped coriander**
**salt and pepper**
**flour**
**1 beaten egg**
**fresh white breadcrumbs**

Melt the butter in a saucepan, toss in the onions and chillies, cover and sweat over a gentle heat for 4-5 minutes. Mix the sweated onions, chillies, mashed potato, fish, coriander, and egg yolk in a bowl and season well with salt and pepper.

Form the mixture into fish cakes about 50g each. Coat them first in flour, then in beaten egg, and finally in breadcrumbs. Chill in the fridge for about 30 minutes (this makes them firmer and easier to cope with) . Then, get your frying pan/griddle really hot and put a little butter in the pan and make sure the butter covers all the surface of the pan. Place the fish cakes on the pan and turn over when golden. Turn down the heat to medium and cook for a further 5 minutes.

# Clodagh McKenna's Baked Haddock with Lemon and Dill

Serves: 4, Preparation time: 5 minutes, Cooking time: 10 - 15 minutes

**2 fillets of haddock**
**1 lemon**
**2 sprigs of dill**
**2 knobs of butter**
**Salt and pepper**

Place the fish on a rectangle of foil and season with salt and pepper.

Squeeze the juice of the lemon between the two fillets, place a sprig of dill on each one and a knob of butter.

Gather all four sides of the foil together to form a tent-like shape and place on a hot barbecue for about ten minutes.

Alternatively place in an oven preheated to 180°C for 10-15 minutes

Serve with a barbecue baked potato and sour cream, or with a big green salad and tomatoes with fresh mint.

# Una McGlynn's Satisfying Seafood Chowder

This tasty rich chowder is a must for all seafood lovers!

Serves: 6 - 8
Preparation time: 15 minutes
Cooking time: 40 minutes

**1lb mixed fresh fish (e.g. salmon, monkfish, mussels,
  smoked coley or suitable available combination)**
**3 cups of white wine**
**2 cups of water**
**2 oz butter**
**drizzle of olive oil**
**1 finely chopped leek**
**2 finely diced carrots**
**2 large garlic cloves (crushed)**
**¼ cup of Pernod**
**½ cup of flour**
**salt and pepper**
**1 pint of cream**
**4 medium potatoes, finely diced**

Part cook the fish for 3-4 minutes in simmering white wine and water. Remove the fish, leaving to cool, and reduce the liquid to use as stock.

Melt butter and olive oil, fry off the leeks for 1-2 minutes. Add the carrots and sweat over a low heat (5-6 minutes) until soft.

Add the garlic to the pan and then the Pernod (this alcohol enhances the fish flavours, but does not overpower the fish), leaving it to bubble down for a minute or two.

Add the flour and allow to cook a little before adding the reduced stock a little at a time, and allow to thicken.

Next, add the potatoes and leave the whole dish to simmer and cook for about 10-15 minutes.

Season to taste. Meanwhile, flake the fish, discarding any skin and bones.

When the potatoes are soft, and just before serving, add the cream and fish and bring to the brink of boiling.

Serve the chowder with a selection of fresh breads for a complete and satisfying meal, or in small portions as a winter warming starter.

COLLIN'S SUPERVALU, BLARNEY
NOMINATED LOCAL CHARITY: MARYMOUNT HOSPICE

# Barry Cullen's Chilli Fish Soup with Mushrooms

This recipe is a variation on a Chilean fish stew which I always enjoy.

Serves: 4
Preparation time: 15 minutes
Cooking time: 50 minutes

**2 tbsp olive oil**
**large knob of butter**
**1lb finely chopped mushrooms**
**1 finely chopped medium onion**
**1 tbsp chopped fresh thyme**
**1 tbsp paprika**
**1 finely chopped chilli**
**2 sliced red peppers**
**4 stalks celery, roughly chopped**
**1L fish stock**
**4 medium potatoes, peeled and sliced**
**4-6 fillets (about 400g) white fish**
**1 tbsp chopped fresh parsley**
**salt and pepper to taste**

Heat oil and butter in a saucepan. When melted and sizzling add mushrooms, onions, thyme and paprika. Stir for 30 seconds.
Lower heat, cover and leave to sweat gently for 15 minutes
Add chilli, red peppers, celery and fish stock; bring to the boil then leave to simmer for 10 minutes.
Add potatoes and simmer for a further 15 minutes.
Add fish, parsley, salt and pepper. When fish is cooked (less than 10 minutes) remove from the heat and serve.

WALLACE'S SUPERVALU, WELLINGTONBRIDGE
NOMINATED LOCAL CHARITY: FRIENDS OF WEXFORD HOSPITAL

# Rosaleen Hindle's Quick and Easy Smoked Mackerel Pate

I always bring some of this along when we go visiting. It can be served as a starter or just as a snack. It's perfect with salad or just with crackers.

Serves: 6 - 8
Preparation time: 5 minutes
Cooking time: 10 minutes

**1 onion, finely chopped**
**1 clove of garlic, crushed**
**5 oz butter**
**½ lb of smoked mackerel, skinned and chopped**
**juice of ½ lemon**
**pinch of ground mace or nutmeg (optional)**
**¼ pint of fresh cream**

Sauté the onion and crushed garlic in butter until the onion is soft.

Add the chopped skinned mackerel, lemon juice, mace and fresh cream, and simmer gently for 5-6 minutes.

Blend this together with a hand blender and then pour into a small container and leave to cool.

Refrigerate until required, and serve spread generously on hot toast.

CAULFIELD'S SUPERVALU, LOUGHBOY
NOMINATED LOCAL CHARITY: KILKENNY SOS

# Anne Marie O'Mahony's Breaded Monk Fish

This delicious dish is easy to cook and will make your guests think you have completed a cordon bleu course in cookery!

Serves: 2
Preparation time: 10 minutes
Cooking time: 20 - 25 minutes

**2 fillets of monk fish**
**1 egg**
**1 tsp of curry powder**
**salt and pepper to season**
**2 cups of breadcrumbs**
**sweet chilli sauce**

**serve with:**
**new baby potatoes and asparagus**

Dry the monk fish with kitchen roll.

Beat the egg and put aside for a moment.

Add the curry, salt and pepper to the bread crumbs (I put these in a small plastic bag and shake well).

Place a baking wire over a baking tray – preheat in an oven at 180°C.

Now dip the monk fish in the beaten egg. When it is well covered roll it in the bread crumb mix and place on the wire tray, repeat for the other fillet.

Cook in the oven for 20-25 minutes, turning once, and sprinkling with any left over breadcrumbs.

Meanwhile, heat the sweet chilli sauce and place in a small bowl.

Serve the monkfish with new baby potatoes and asparagus with the sweet chilli sauce to the side.

RYAN'S SUPERVALU, GLANMIRE
NOMINATED LOCAL CHARITY: TIR NA N'ÓG RESPITE SERVICES

# Susan Jane Murray's Mum's Potato Cakes

Irish spuds are magical. So is my mum. Monday's a good day for potato cakes – it's a useful way to use leftovers from Sunday dinner.

Serves: 4 large or 8 small cakes
Preparation time: 10 minutes
Cooking time: 10 minutes

**4 cups mashed potato**
**1 egg**
**¼ cup of flour**
**2 spring onions**
**Herbamere seasoning**

**flaked salmon**
**garlic, crushed**
**coriander, freshly chopped**

Chop the green and white part of the spring onions.

Mash or beat everything together.

Heat a frying pan on high with coconut oil or butter.

When piping hot drop large spoonfuls of mixture onto pan, flatten with the back of a fish-slice.

Turn down heat a little to prevent burning.

Fry both sides until golden (about 3 minutes each side to allow the flour to cook).

Allow to cool, wrap in baking parchment, and munch on the go for a speedy lunch, or serve with your favourite salsa.

The addition of flaked salmon, crushed garlic and freshly chopped coriander makes a tantalising alternative – streets ahead of any fish cakes you'll buy at restaurants. Serve with a royal dollop of natural yoghurt and a pinch of curry powder.

GALLAGHER'S SUPERVALU, WICKLOW
NOMINATED LOCAL CHARITY: WICKLOW HOSPITAL

# Marcella Costello's Crab Soufflé

This recipe is a really great way to impress at a dinner party.

Serves: 4-6
Preparation time: 10 minutes
Cooking time: 20-25 minutes

**150g fresh crab meat**
**25g butter, and extra for greasing**
**25g flour**
**150ml milk**
**4 egg whites**
**3 egg yolks**
**2 tbsp chopped fresh herbs (chives, chervil, parsley, dill**
**salt and pepper**

Tip

A soufflé is quite a courageous dish to try out as ovens vary. Give this one a little trial run before deciding to execute it for a dinner party, and remember don't bang the oven door or they might just sink!

In a pan make a roux by cooking the butter and flour together for a few minutes.

Slowly add the milk to create a really thick but smooth white sauce. Bring to the boil and leave to simmer for 5-6 minutes until really thick.

Remove from the heat and allow to cool slightly.

Meanwhile place the egg whites in a spotlessly clean bowl and whisk to a stiff peak.

Now beat the egg yolks into the slightly cooled sauce mixture, season, add the fresh chopped herbs and the crab meat, mix well.

Gently fold the beaten egg whites into this mixture taking care not to over mix.

Butter 4-6 little ramekins or oven proof cups and fill them ⅔ full.

Place in a preheated oven for about 12-15 minutes at 190°C.

Remove the light risen soufflés and serve at once.

With a salad or simply on their own, a soufflé can be a beautiful light lunch or dinner party starter!

# Tom Shanahan's Prawns with Basil and Garlic Butter

This is often served by my sister, who coaxed the recipe from a chef in California.

Serves: 4
Preparation time: 10 minutes
Cooking time: 10 minutes

**12 jumbo prawns**
**salt and pepper**
**1½ tbsp olive oil**
**2 tsp crushed garlic**
**80ml dry white wine**
**1 tbsp lemon juice**
**2 tbsp chopped sundried tomatoes**
**6 oz butter**
**2 oz shredded fresh basil**

Preheat the oven to 180°C/350°F/Gas 4

Season the prawns with salt and pepper.

Heat oil in a large non stick frying pan over moderate heat until hot but not smoking.

Sauté prawns for 1 minute per side.

Transfer prawns to a baking dish and bake in the middle of the oven until just cooked through (about 7 minutes).

Meanwhile add the garlic to the pan and cook, stirring, over a moderate heat for 15 seconds, then stir in wine, lemon juice and tomatoes.

Boil, stirring occasionally until the liquid is reduced by two-thirds.

Swirl in butter and basil over a low heat and season well with salt and pepper.

Serve the sauce poured generously over the prawns, with crusty bread for mopping.

This serves 4 as a starter. To serve as a main course simply increase the quantity as required

MORRISSEY'S SUPERVALU, CASHEL
NOMINATED LOCAL CHARITY: SOUTH TIPPERARY HOSPICE, CASHEL

# Grace O'Shea's Salmon and Broccoli Quiche

This is a variation on your classic quiche. Being a fish lover I experimented with salmon and I'm glad I did – it goes down a treat!

Serves: 6
Preparation time: 15 minutes and chilling time
Cooking time: 55 minutes

**For the pastry:**
200g plain flour
60g margarine
20g finely grated light cheddar cheese
cold water
1 dsp mixed herbs
salt

**For the filling:**
250g cooked salmon, boned and broken into
  bite size pieces
75g fresh broccoli, divided into small florets and
  precooked for 5 minutes
4 medium free range eggs
200ml fresh cream
40g grated light cheddar cheese
2 tbsp fresh tarragon, finely chopped
sea salt and pepper

Place the flour in a mixing bowl and season with salt and herbs.

Rub the margarine into the flour until it resembles fine breadcrumbs. Mix in the grated cheese

Add enough cold water to make a stiff dough. Wrap in cling film and chill for at least 1 hour.

Remove from fridge, discard cling film and roll onto a floured surface. Press into a greased quiche dish

Bake blind in a preheated oven at 200°C for 10 minutes. Remove and allow to cool slightly. Reduce temperature to 170°C.

Meanwhile whisk the eggs with the cream, season with salt, pepper and tarragon.

Scatter the salmon and broccoli over the base of the pastry case. Pour the egg mixture over this. Sprinkle grated cheese on top.

Cook for 45 minutes. Allow to cool slightly before serving. Enjoy with a fresh side salad.

MURPHY'S SUPERVALU, CASTLETOWNBERE
NOMINATED LOCAL CHARITY: CASTLETOWNBERE RNLI
LIFEBOAT

# Katalin Fekete's Ginger and Honey Glazed Fish Skewers

This is one of my mum's gourmet recipes. Perfect for summer evenings or family gatherings.

Serves: 2
Preparation time: 10 minutes
Cooking time: 10 minutes

**3 lb cod or salmon fillets, cubed**
**1 yellow pepper, cut into large chunks**
**1 green pepper, cut into large chunks**
**1 tsp ground ginger**
**1 tbsp honey**
**juice of half a lemon**
**zest of half a lemon**
**1 tsp fresh parsley, finely chopped**
**salt and ground black pepper**
**bamboo skewers**

Mix all the ingredients in a bowl, excluding the fish and peppers to make a creamy seasoning.

Thread 1 fish chunk, then 1 pepper chunk onto the skewers.

Repeat until the skewer is full.

Apply the creamy seasoning with a brush to the skewers.

Grill gently until the fish is cooked through.

Serve with a potato salad.

CAULFIELD'S SUPERVALU, MALAHIDE
NOMINATED LOCAL CHARITY: CASA - CARING AND
SHARING ASSOCIATION, MALAHIDE

# Edward Brian Fawcett's Cod Au Gratin

I used to fish in the North Sea and so had a regular supply of fresh cod. This is my favourite cod dish – it tastes great!

Serves: 2
Preparation time: 10 minutes
Cooking time: 10 minutes

**30g butter**
**2 x 300g tail end cod fillets (no bones!)**
**100g button mushrooms, sliced finely**
**300ml white sauce plus a 'glug' of white wine**
**50g grated cheddar cheese**
**20g dried breadcrumbs**

Heat the butter in a frying pan and then fry cod for 2 minutes on each side.

Season well and then arrange in a gratin dish.

Add mushrooms, white sauce and wine to the frying pan, stir for 1 minute and then pour on top of the fish in the gratin dish.

Cover with grated cheese and sprinkle with breadcrumbs.

Dot with butter and place under a hot grill until golden brown.

KANE AND MCCARTNEY'S SUPERVALU, DROGHEDA
NOMINATED LOCAL CHARITY: ST VINCENT DE PAUL,
DROGHEDA

# Caroline Cronin's Plaice and Orange

I'm lucky to have an abundance of fresh fish on my doorstep — I love this easy recipe and so do my kids!

Serves: 2
Preparation time: 5 minutes
Cooking time: 15-25 minutes

**1 small orange, peeled**
**1 red pepper (seeded and halved)**
**4 oz cottage cheese**
**4 plaice fillets, skinned**
**juice and rind of one orange**
**butter**
**parsley**

Half the orange and the pepper. Chop up half of each and keep the other half for garnishing.

Combine the pepper, orange, cottage cheese together.

Divide this mixture between the four place fillets and roll up.

Place in a casserole dish, pour over the orange juice and orange rind, and add a few knobs of butter.

Cover and bake in a moderate oven for 15-25 minutes, basting occasionally.

Garnish with parsley and serve with your favourite accompaniments.

FIELD'S SUPERVALU, SKIBBEREEN
NOMINATED LOCAL CHARITY: COPE FOUNDATION, SKIBBEREEN

# Clodagh McKenna's Zesty Tuna

Serves: 4
Preparation time: 10 minutes (plus 1 hour to marinate)
Cooking time: 5 minutes

**225g fresh tuna loin**
**2 limes, juice and zest**
**2 cloves of garlic, crushed**
**1 tbsp of fresh coriander, chopped**
**1 red chilli, finely chopped**
**4 tbsp olive oil**
**salt and freshly ground black pepper**

Slice the tuna loin into slices about an inch thick.

In a bowl mix the lime, garlic, fresh coriander, chilli, and olive oil, then season with salt and pepper to make a marinade.

Once the marinade is well mixed add in the tuna, cover and place in a fridge. Leave to marinate for an hour.

Remove from the fridge and take out the tuna, keeping aside the remaining marinade if cooking in a pan.

On a barbecue or frying pan, cook the tuna on each side for 30 seconds.

If cooking in a pan remove the cooked tuna and add the marinade to the pan and allow to bubble for 2-3 minutes, then pour this over the tuna.

Serve with a big bowl of salad or boiled rice.

DEDICATED TO: DORAN'S SUPERVALU, GRAIGUENAMAGH
NOMINATED LOCAL CHARITY: GAHAN HOUSE HOME (FOR THE ELDERLY)

# Claire King's Creamy Smoked Fish Pasta

This is a simple but really tasty recipe. It's a great comforter on a cold dreary day.

Serves: 4
Preparation time: 20 minutes
Cooking time: 25 minutes

**Smoked fish (cod or haddock) – enough to serve 4**
**1 carton of double cream**
**1 glass white wine**
**2 leeks, chopped**
**1 medium onion, chopped**
**1-2 cloves garlic, crushed (depending on your taste)**
**handful of mushrooms**
**1 pack of tagliatelle pasta (enough to serve 4)**

Wrap the fish in tin foil and place in a preheated oven at 200°C/400°F/Gas Mark 6 for 20 minutes.

Fry the onion and garlic over a low heat for 5 minutes, then add the leeks and mushrooms.

Boil a pan of water and add the tagliatelle.

When the fish is cooked, chop into cubes and add to the vegetables in the pan. Add the wine and cream and season well.

Continue to cook over a low heat for 5 minutes.

Serve with the sauce spooned over the tagliatelle, and some crusty bread on the side.

MURPHY'S SUPERVALU, CARRICK-ON-SUIR
NOMINATED LOCAL CHARITY: LOCAL ST. VINCENT DE. PAUL SOCIETY

# Imelda Hehir's Fish en Papiotte

My friend and I got the idea from a restaurant and made a few changes – it's always the way we cook fish now!!

Serves: 2
Preparation time: 10 minutes
Cooking time: 20 minutes

**1 lb fresh fish**
**zest and juice of one lemon**
**1 shallot**
**a few strips of peppers and courgette**
**1 clove garlic, crushed**
**¼ cup white wine**
**1 tbsp olive oil**
**1 tsp fresh chopped thyme**
**salt and pepper to taste**

Take two sheets of parchment paper and lay on top of each other.

Fold over one end of sheets to create one large sheet.
Drizzle the olive oil in the middle of paper.

Place fish on paper and season with salt and pepper to taste
Combine all other ingredients in bowl and mix together and reserve.

Take ends of paper and fold over to create pouch (I use stapler for a better seal).

Leave opening on top to pour reserved ingredients
Close the pouch and staple. Bake in preheated 200°C oven for 20-25 minutes.

Remove from oven and carefully open top of pouch.

Steam will be present in the pouch so please be careful!.

Serving suggestions: Great to serve with couscous, brown rice, or roasted potato. Asparagus and sugar snap peas make ideal accompaniments.

NESTOR'S SUPERVALU, BALLYBANE
NOMINATED LOCAL CHARITY: GALWAY HOSPICE

# Liesl Viglino's Brown Rice Paella

A delicious Paella dish perfect for sharing

Serves: 4
Preparation time: 30 minutes
Cooking time: 40 minutes

**1 cup of brown rice cooked in vegetable stock**
**1 onion**
**1 red pepper**
**1 green pepper**
**1 tbsp crushed garlic**
**2 cardamom seeds and aniseed pods**
**½ tomato, put in hot water to remove the skin**
**1 pkt of New Zealand mussels**
**1 pkt prawns**
**3 joints of smoked chicken**
**5 Kielbasa sausages, chopped or other Spanish sausage**
**1 pkt seafood mix**
**Frozen peas and corn**

Fry chopped onion, garlic, tomato, peppers.

Crush cardamom seed and aniseed pod to release flavour. Add to onion and garlic mix. Mix in the cooked brown rice.

Steam the mussels and set aside.

Steam the prawns and seafood mix.

Preheat the oven to 350° F/ 180° C/ Gas 4 and roast the smoked chicken.

Microwave the Kielbasa for a minute on a high power, or cook the spanish sausage.

Steam the peas and corn.

Mix everything together except the chicken.

Place the chicken on top of the rice mix and season as required.

KENNA'S SUPERVALU, MAYNOOTH
NOMINATED LOCAL CHARITY: CRUMLIN HOSPITAL

# Chef Aongus Hanly's Cod fillets in Serrano Ham with green Lentils

The combination of these simple ingredients really bring a tasty piece of Cod to life!

Serves: 4
Preparation time: 5 minutes
Cooking time: 10 minutes

**4 x 175g fillets of cod**
**4 slices of Serrano ham (alternatively use streaky bacon)**
**2 tsp olive oil**
**1 large clove of garlic (finely chopped)**
**2 x 400g tins of green lentils (drained)**
**salt and pepper**

Pre-heat the oven to 200°C. Season the Cod fillets lightly and wrap each of them in a slice of Serrano ham.

Put the wrapped Cod on an oven tray brushed with a teaspoon of olive oil. Place the tray in the oven and cook for 10 minutes (or a little longer if the fillets are thick) until cooked.

While the cod is cooking, lightly cook the chopped garlic with the remaining teaspoon of olive oil in a small sauce pan. Add the drained lentils and heat through. Season to taste.

When the cod is cooked serve each fillet with a spoonful of lentils.

DEDICATED TO: KELLEHER'S SUPERVALU, CAPPOQUINN
NOMINATED LOCAL CHARITY: WEST WATERFORD
HOSPICE

# Chef Hugh McNally's Pan Fried Pollock fillets with Leek Fondue

Serves: 4
Preparation time: 5 minutes
Cooking time: 15 minutes

**40g butter**
**2 large leeks very finely chopped**
**½ tsp curry powder**
**4 tbsp of dry white wine**
**200ml single cream**
**4 x 5oz fillets of pollock**
**3 tbsp of olive oil**
**salt and pepper**

Heat the butter in a pan and gently cook the leeks in it until soft but not coloured (this takes approximately 5-7 minutes).

Just when the leeks are almost cooked add in the curry powder and stir in well.

Now stir in the wine and cook for a further 2 minutes. Season and pour in the cream.

Meanwhile, simmer for 5 minutes so the liquid reduces. Keep the fondue of leeks warm.

Season the pollock fillets and fry in a pan with the olive oil for 2 – 3 minutes on each side. Drain on kitchen paper towels.

Spoon small moulds of the leek fondue on a plate and place the pollock fillets on top and serve immediately.

DEDICATED TO: LANNEY'S SUPERVALU, ARDEE
NOMINATED LOCAL CHARITY: ARDEE HOSPICE

# Chef Hugh McNally's
# Darne of Caramelised Lime Salmon

Serves: 4
Preparation time: 10 minutes
Cooking time: 10 minutes

**2 tsp of vegetable oil**
**4 x 5oz salmon darnes with skin on**
**2 tbsp of lime juice**
**3 tbsp of brown sugar**
**1 tsp of Asian fish sauce**
**1 tbsp of soy sauce**
**1 tsp of chilli flakes**
**1 cucumber sliced into ribbons (use a vegetable peeler**
  **or mandolin for this)**
**½ cup of coriander**
**bunch of sliced spring onion**

Heat a non stick pan and put in the vegetable oil. Place the salmon in the pan, flesh side down.

Cook the salmon for 2 - 3 min on each side.

Combine all the other ingredients (except the coriander and spring onions) and add this to the fish when it has been cooked. Reduce this mixture until it becomes just slightly sticky. This should take approximately 3 - 4 minutes.

Place the coriander leaves in the centre of each serving plate. Sit the salmon on top and place the cucumber to the side. Drizzle the surplus liquid around the plate and serve.

DEDICATED TO: MCDONNELL'S SUPERVALU, SANTRY
NOMINATED LOCAL CHARITY: ST MICHAEL'S HOUSE

# Chef Hugh McNally's
# Sea Bass Fillets with Gremolata Dressing

Serves: 4
Preparation time: 10 minutes + 2 hours standing time
Cooking time: 5 minutes

**4 sea bass fillets, with skin on**
**4 tbsp of olive oil**

**For the Gremolata:**
**large bunch of flat parsley, finely chopped**
**grated zest of 1 Lemon**
**½ tsp of sea salt**
**1 red chilli, deseeded, finely chopped**
**1 shallot, finely chopped**
**olive oil**
**salt and pepper**

For the gremolata, you mix all the ingredients in a bowl. Add enough olive oil until a very loose paste is formed.

You should make this dressing a couple of hours in advance to allow the flavours to develop.

Heat a non stick pan and season the sea bass fillets. Add the olive oil and cook the fillets skin side down for 2-3 minutes until the skin is crisp and golden brown, then turn over and cook for another minute of two until just cooked through.

Plate the sea bass and spoon the Gremolata dressing over it until the fish is coated in it.

DEDICATED TO: DOOLEY'S SUPERVALU,
FORTUNESTOWN, TALLAGHT
NOMINATED LOCAL CHARITY: LOCAL ST. VINCENT DE PAUL

# Anne Walsh's Fish Bake

This is a delicious dish that always goes down well with my family! It's easy to make, doesn't take a lot of preparation and is a healthy choice for your family.

Serves: 4
Preparation time: 10 minutes
Cooking time: 35-40 minutes

**400g selection of vegetables such as peppers, red onions, mushrooms, leeks and celery**
**1 tbsp olive oil**
**4 x 175g portions fleshy boned white fish such as cod or whiting**
**4 fresh tomatoes, chopped**
**sea salt and black pepper**

Chop your preferred vegetables. Toss in olive oil, season and roast in an oven for 15-20 minutes at 400°F/ 200°C/ Gas 6.

Wash and dry the fish portions and season well with sea salt and black pepper.

Place the fish on top of the pre roasted vegetables.

Place the chopped tomatoes on top of the fish.

Return to the oven and continue to cook for about 15-20 minutes until the fish is cooked through.

Serve with potatoes and/or fresh green salad.

RYAN'S SUPERVALU, BALLYHAUNIS
NOMINATED LOCAL CHARITY: MAYO ROSSCOMMON HOSPICE

# Clodagh Murphy's Mackerel Baked in Foil

A quick and easy Mackerel dish that tastes delicious.

Serves: 2
Preparation time: 10 minutes
Cooking time: 25 minutes

**2 whole mackerel, cleaned and gutted**
**1 lemon**
**2 sprigs fresh rosemary**
**2 cloves of garlic**
**1 red onion, sliced**
**4 tbsp cider**
**black pepper and sea salt**

Preheat oven to 200°C.

Place mackerel on a large square of baking paper. Set on a square of tin foil. Season with salt and pepper.

Cut lemon into slices. Place lemon slices inside each fish cavity with the rosemary and garlic.

Scatter the onion and drizzle the cider over the fish.

Wrap the tin foil and baking paper loosely around each fish, securing the edges to make a parcel and bake for 25 minutes.

Serve with boiled potatoes and parsley.

KEANE'S SUPERVALU, KILLORGLIN
NOMINATED LOCAL CHARITY: THE AISLING GROUP

# Joan Clancy's Grilled Salmon Teriyaki with Mushrooms

A very simple, easy to prepare feast that's sure to impress!

Serves: 2
Preparation time: 20 minutes (plus 20 minutes marinating)
Cooking time: 20-25 minutes

**2 x 175g salmon darnes, skin on**
**2 tsp olive oil**
**1 garlic clove, crushed**
**2 tbsp Teriyaki sauce**
**juice of 1 lime or ½ lemon**
**sea salt and coarsely ground black pepper**
**a few knobs of butter**

**For the mushrooms:**
**225g (½ lb mushrooms)**
**1 tbsp butter**
**2 cloves crushed garlic**
**1 stick celery, diced**
**1 small carrot, sliced using a potato peeler**
**1 finely diced large potato**
**1 chicken stock cube, crumbled**
**250ml carton of cream**
**dash of white pepper**

Place a large sheet of tin foil on a baking sheet and drizzle a teaspoon of oil over it.

Place the salmon darnes on the foil, flesh side up.

Combine the remaining teaspoon of olive oil with the garlic, Teriyaki sauce and the juice of the lime (or lemon) and pour over the fish. Seal the foil loosely and leave to marinate for at least 20 minutes, overnight if possible.

Preheat grill to the highest setting. Carefully open foil and spoon juices over the fish. Sprinkle with salt and pepper, and add the knobs of butter.

Place the baking sheet with open tin foil packages under the hot grill for about 6-8 minutes until golden, basting with juices regularly.

Meanwhile, to make the creamy mushrooms: Roughly cut the mushrooms and place in a saucepan with all the remaining ingredients. Seal with a tight fitting lid and bring to the boil, stirrring.

Simmer slowly for 10-15 minutes, stir and serve with the salmon.

MORRISSEY'S SUPERVALU, DUNGARVAN
NOMINATED LOCAL CHARITY: FRIENDS OF ST. JOSEPH'S
HOSPICE, DUNGARVAN

# Michael English's Bouillabaisse

This is a mouth watering traditional Provencal fish stew which has its roots in Marseilles.

Preparation time: 20 minutes
Cooking time: 50 minutes

**2 lb mixed fish**
**1 lb shell fish**
**1 onion, sliced**
**1 carrot, sliced**
**1 stick celery**
**1 bay leaf**
**6 tsp olive oil**
**3 strips orange peel**
**4 tomatoes, skinned and chopped**
**2 small leeks, trimmed and finely chopped**
**2 small cloves of garlic, finely chopped**
**a good pinch of saffron threads**
**1 sprig fresh thyme**
**salt and pepper**
**2 ½ pints water**

To make the stock: Clean and prepare fish by removing skin and bones, and cut into chunks. Shellfish can be left in their shells.

Put the fish trimmings and bones into a large pan with the onion, celery, carrot and bay leaf.

Add 2 ½ pints of water and bring to the boil. Add salt and pepper, remove any scum that rises, cover and simmer for 30 minutes. Strain and reserve the stock.

To make the soup; heat oil in a pan and add garlic and leeks, then cook over a low heat for 5 minutes

Add tomatoes and cook for 5 minutes, then pour in the stock and bring to the boil

Stir in orange peel, saffron and thyme. When boiling add white fish and simmer for 8 minutes

Add shellfish and cook for 5 minutes. Season to taste, then serve

HENEGHAN'S SUPERVALU, GLENAMADDY
NOMINATED LOCAL CHARITY: GRÁ IN LOUGHREA - PARENT
SUPPORT GROUP FOR CHILDREN WITH AUTISM

# Chef Hugh McNally's Fish Pie

This delicious rich fish pie is sure to get mouths watering!

Serves: 4
Preparation time: 15 minutes
Cooking time: 1 hour 15 minutes

**25g unsalted butter**
**800g seafood mix (smoked coley, cod fillets, prawns, mussels), cut into bite sized pieces**
**500ml fish stock**
**4 shallots, peeled and finely chopped**
**250ml white wine**
**250ml dry Martini**
**500ml double cream**
**1 lemon, halved**
**salt and pepper**
**few sprigs of fresh tarragon and flat parsley**
**5 large Desiree potatoes, diced**
**1 egg yolk**
**a little milk and butter**

Heat Butter in a Saucepan and gently sweat the shallots until soft.

Add the wine and Martini and simmer slowly until liquid is reduced by half.

Now add the stock and again reduce the liquid by half. Stir in the cream and continue to reduce until the liquid has a consistency similar to pouring cream.

Boil the Potatoes until tender, mash and add the butter, milk and the egg yolk. Meanwhile, season the sauce and strain through a sieve to collect the shallots.

Season the fish and add to the sauce with a squeeze of lemon juice and the parsley and tarragon.

Pour the whole mixture into an earthenware dish. Preheat the oven to 180°C.

Pipe or spoon the mash onto the fish and place in the oven for 20 minutes until bubbling and golden brown.

DEDICATED TO: DUNNE'S SUPERVALU, BALLINASLOE
NOMINATED LOCAL CHARITY: THE AISLING GROUP

# Chef Hugh McNally's
# Herb Crust Fillet of Hake with Classic Aioli

Serves 4
Preparation: 20 minutes
Cooking time: 10-12 minutes

**4 5oz Fillets of Fresh Hake**
**250g Fresh Breadcrumbs**
**4 Table spoons olive oil**
**1 finely chopped Shallot**
**30g Finely grated Parmesan**
**3 sprigs of finely chopped coriander and chives**

**For the Aioli**
**teaspoon Safffon (optional)**
**2 tablespoons water**
**2 egg yolks**
**2 cloves of pureed garlic**
**½ teaspoon Tabasco sauce**
**Cup of olive oil**
**½ the juice from a lemon**
**Salt and Pepper**

For the Aioli steep the Saffron in the 2 tablespoons of water for 5 min.

Combine the egg yolks, garlic, tobasco, salt and pepper and lemon juice in a food processor.

Add the steeped saffron and water. Add in the olive oil very slowly until an emulsion is formed and your Aioli is ready.

Pre Heat the Oven to 180°C.

For the Herb crust sauté the chopped shallot in a tablespoon of olive oil for about 3 minutes without colouring. Remove from the heat and add in the bread crumbs and chopped herbs and Parmesan. Mix with a fork and add more oil to moisten if needed.

Generously top each of the Hake fillets with the herb crust.

In a hot pan place the hake fillet crust side down and cook for 3 minutes until breadcrumbs begin to get crisry and brown. Turn fillet over and continue to cook for 4-5 min.

Place Hake on a plate with some buttered cooked vegetables and surround with a little of the Aioli.

DEDICATED TO: DICK'S SUPERVALU, BALLYRAGGET
NOMINATED LOCAL CHARITY: NEW HORIZONS, SCHOOL
FOR AUTISM, GORESBRIDGE

# Eithne Conway's Mediterranean Style Cod

I tried a dish similar to this while on holiday in Malta. I loved the flavour so much that I tried to recreate it when I returned home – this is the result!

Serves: 4
Preparation time: 20 minutes
Cooking time: 15-20 minutes

**900g (2lbs) fresh cod, skinned, boned and chopped into 1½ inch cubes**
**1 large onion, finely chopped**
**3 cloves of garlic, finely chopped**
**2 tbsp of sunflower oil**
**A good sprinkle of dried oregano or basil**
**2 tins of chopped tomatoes**
**100g (4oz) fresh breadcrumbs**
**130g (5oz) grated red cheddar**
**1 tbsp fresh chopped parsley**

Heat the oil in a frying pan and gently fry the onion and garlic for two minutes

Add a decent sprinkle of dried oregano or basil and cook for another minute

Then add the tinned tomatoes, heat through and simmer gently for ten minutes

Remove from the heat and gently fold in the chopped cod. Transfer to a casserole dish

Mix the breadcrumbs, fresh chopped parsley and red cheddar, and sprinkle this mixture over the top of the pie

Bake at 180°C for 15-20 minutes until the pie is a warm golden colour on top

Serve with new potatoes and freshly steamed broccoli

QUISH'S SUPERVALU, BALLINCOLLIG
NOMINATED LOCAL CHARITY: GUIDE DOGS ASSOCIATION

# Vegetable
Recipes

# Clodagh McKenna's Beetroot Hummus

Great served as a dip with lots of seasonal vegetables sliced up and served raw or also as a filler for a toasted pitta.

Makes approx. 500g
Preparation time: 10 minutes
Cooking time: 30 minutes

**2 fresh beetroots**
**60ml (2fl oz) olive oil**
**2 garlic cloves, peeled**
**420g (15oz) cooked, canned chickpeas**
**juice of 1 lemon**
**salt and freshly ground**
**black pepper**

Put the whole uncooked beetroot in a saucepan with a little water and leave to cook for approx. 25 minutes depending on how big they are.

You can test to see if they are cooked by pushing back the skin with your thumb, if the skin comes off easily then the beetroots are cooked.

Once the beetroots are cooked, peel the skin off and chop them up roughly.

Then place the garlic, beetroot and chickpeas in a food processor and whiz until well blended.

Then add the lemon juice and drizzle in the remaining olive oil through the feed tube to make a fairly coarse paste.

Season to taste and spoon into a serving bowl.

DEDICATED TO: REGAN'S SUPERVALU, FIRHOUSE
NOMINATED LOCAL CHARITY: HAROLD'S CROSS HOSPICE

# Clodagh McKenna's Summer Insalata Riso

This is a really popular salad in Italy, all the ingredients are readily available in Ireland so it's a perfect salad for here to!

Serves: 4
Preparation time: 20 minutes
Cooking time: 25 minutes

**100g rice (basmati or wild)**
**50g peas (fresh or frozen)**
**50g sweetcorn**
**100g cherry tomatoes (halved)**
**2 hard boiled eggs**
**juice of 1 lemon**
**extra virgin olive oil**
**salt and pepper**

Firstly cook the rice by rinsing then boiling in water for 15-20 minutes, then rinse with hot water and leave to cool.

When cooled place the rice in a large bowl and mix in the sweetcorn, pea's and halved cherry tomatoes.

Cut the hardboiled eggs into quarters, then half again and toss into the rice.

Add in a slurp of extra virgin olive oil, juice of 1 lemon, season with salt and pepper and mix well.

DEDICATED TO: CUMMINS' SUPERVALU, BALLINROBE
NOMINATED LOCAL CHARITY: WESTERN CARE

# Jonathan Sultan's Sweet Potato Soup with Walnuts, Apple and Cider

This simple soup is heartwarming and healthy – the children love it on cold days

Serves: 4
Preparation time: 15 minutes
Cooking time: 1½ minutes

**Soup:**
2 oz butter
1 large onion, chopped
1 carrot, chopped
1 apple, peeled, cored and chopped
1 sprig fresh thyme
1 bay leaf
1 pint dry cider
1 lb sweet potatoes (peeled and chopped)
2 pints chicken stock

**To Garnish:**
2 oz butter
1 apple, peeled, cored and diced
2 oz walnuts
1 oz brown sugar
4 fl oz whipped cream
4 sprigs chervil

To make the soup, melt the butter in a thick bottomed saucepan over a medium heat

Add the onion, carrot, bay leaf and thyme. Sweat for a few minutes until the onion turns translucent

Add the cider and boil vigorously until the cider has reduced by half

Add the sweet potato and chicken stock. Season with salt and pepper

Bring to the boil and then simmer until the potatoes are cooked (about 1 hour)

Remove the herbs and puree the soup in a blender. You can then pass through a fine sieve if you wish. Taste and season if necessary

While the soup is cooking sauté the diced apple and walnuts in butter over a high heat

Add the brown sugar when the apple is beginning to colour. Cook until the apple has turned golden

To serve, ladle the soup into warm bowls. Place a spoon of whipped cream in the centre and sprinkle with a little of the apple and walnuts

Finish each soup with a sprig of chervil

KIERNAN'S SUPERVALU, MOUNT MERRION
NOMINATED LOCAL CHARITY: MOUNT MERRION
COMMUNITY CENTRE

# Pat Wynne's Potato Bites

Children love these, and they also make a great starter when served with a dipping sauce — great as they can be made the day before!

Serves: 4 - 5
Preparation time: 15 minutes
Cooking time: 5 minutes

**8 oz cooked, mashed potato**
**4 oz cheddar cheese**
**2 tbsp parsley**
**2 oz flour**
**1 egg, beaten**
**Breadcrumbs to coat**

**Dipping sauce:**
**2 large tomatoes**
**1 onion**
**¼ pint of stock**
**1 tsp brown sugar**

Mix potato, grated cheese and parsley

Roll into small balls

Coat each ball in flour, followed by egg, followed by breadcrumbs

Deep fry until golden and drain on kitchen paper

To make the sauce: chop the tomato, fry the onion and add the stock. Add sugar to taste. Pureé until smooth

Serve the bites with a ramekin of dipping sauce on the side

KELLY'S SUPERVALU, BOYLE
NOMINATED LOCAL CHARITY: LOURDES INVALID FUND

# Susan McDonald's Stuffed Peppers

A fantastic healthy, and filling, main meal that I make on a weekly basis. It's brilliant for kids and very easy to prepare.

Serves: 4
Preparation time: 20 minutes
Cooking time: 30 minutes

**4 peppers**
**4 oz sunflower seeds**
**2 tsp whole grain mustard**
**1 x 200ml tub of crème fraîche**
**1 bunch spring onions, chopped**
**4 oz Gruyere cheese, grated**
**4 tbsp coriander, chopped (optional)**
**Loaf of bread, blitzed in a food processor to make breadcrumbs**
**6 oz Parma ham, chopped (optional)**
**salt and pepper**

Wash peppers and chop off the tops. Scoop out seeds and rinse insides out well

Stand peppers up on a baking tray (cutting a thin sliver off the end to help with balance).

Mix all other ingredients together in a bowl

Fill each pepper to the top with the mixture

Bake at in a pre-heated oven 180°C for 30 minutes

Delicious served with salad and garlic bread

Tip
If you don't want to go vegetarian for dinner simply add the parma ham to the mix

MCINERNEY'S SUPERVALU, LOUGHREA
NOMINATED LOCAL CHARITY: CANCER CARE WEST

# Fíana Reid's Mediterranean Bean Stew

I love 'mop up' food and I cook this dish for vegetarian friends. It's a twist on four meat dishes!

Serves: 2 - 3
Preparation time: 15 minutes
Cooking time: 1-1½ hours

**1 red pepper**
**1 yellow pepper**
**8 cloves of garlic**
**8 shallots**
**2 tins of chopped tomatoes**
**1 tin of butter beans**
**Olive oil**
**Black pepper and salt**
**1 dessertspoon soy sauce**
**Handful of black olives, halved**
**A good dash of white or red wine**
**Pinch of oregano**

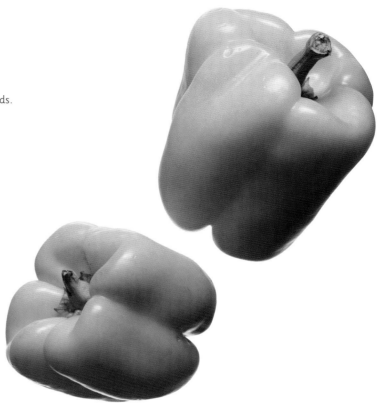

Fry the shallots and peppers in olive oil

Add the wine and stew for ½ an hour

Add the garlic (whole), tomatoes, olives, beans, soy sauce, pepper and salt

Stew this very slowly for about 1 hour – it should be thick and rich

Add the oregano and some olive oil

Serve piping hot with garlic bread or a crisp green salad

CAULFIELD'S SUPERVALU, ENNISCORTHY
NOMINATED LOCAL CHARITY: ARTHRITIS IRELAND IN THE SOUTH EAST

# Niamh Ní Dhúill's Seasonal Vegetable Curry

Beautiful colours and great flavours combine to make this tasty and simple vegetarian dish

Serves: 4
Preparation time: 15 minutes
Cooking time: 30 - 40 minutes

**4 cloves of garlic**
**2 leeks or scallions, chopped**
**1 sweet potato (optional) diced**
**300g organic tomato and vegetable sauce**
**Organic oil**
**2 tsp curry paste (coriander and lemon)**
**100g Mange tout**
**100g purple sprouting broccoli/broccoli/cauliflower**
**200mls sour cream or Glenisk organic natural yoghurt**
**Sprinkle of Japanese seasoning – Furikake (optional)**
**200g mix of chopped herbs (e.g. coriander, rocket, chervil etc.)**
**Juice of ½ lemon**

Heat oil in a saucepan. Add the crushed garlic cloves, then add the leeks

Add the sweet potato and continuously stir

Add the tomato sauce and curry paste

Add the mange tout and broccoli, and cook for 5-7 minutes

Add all of the chopped herbs, seasoning and lemon juice and cook for another 5 minutes

Finally add the sour cream, stir and allow to cook for a final five minutes

Serve with brown basmati rice and garnish with the sprouts

GARVEY'S SUPERVALU, TRALEE
NOMINATED LOCAL CHARITY: TRALEE MS SOCIETY

# Deirdre Shiel's Curried Potato Melt

This evolved from using up leftovers — now a family 'must have'!

Serves: 4 - 6
Preparation time: 10 minutes
Cooking time: 20 - 30 minutes

**2 medium onions, peel and quartered**
**1 clove garlic, peeled**
**4 large cooked potatoes, peeled and quartered**
**2 oz SuperValu plain flour**
**1½ tsp Sharwoods medium curry powder**
**2 large eggs**
**200g grated red cheddar and mozzarella cheese**

Line a 14" x 10" tin with baking parchment.

Preheat the oven to 180°C.

In a food processor, whiz onion and garlic for a few minutes.

Add potatoes and whiz again.

Add flour, curry powder, the eggs and half of the cheese. Whiz again.

Spread evenly on the prepared tin.

Sprinkle the remaining cheese on top.

Bake in the oven for 20-30 minutes until bubbling and brown.

Cut into squares. Great hot, or cold for picnics and lunchboxes.

TOP TIP
For a bit of variety leave out the curry powder and a bit of chopper black pudding or a little more egg for a Spanish omelette

NESTOR'S SUPERVALU, FR GRIFFIN ROAD, GALWAY
NOMINATED LOCAL CHARITY: GALWAY HOSPICE

# Chef Aongus Hanly's Roast Vegetable and Couscous Pie

Beautiful colours and great flavours combine to make this tasty and simple vegetarian dish.

Serves: 4-6
Preparation time: 20-25 minutes
Cooking time: 40-50 minutes

**1 carrot (peeled)**
**1 parsnip (peeled)**
**1 red pepper (seeded)**
**1 yellow pepper (seeded)**
**1 green pepper (seeded)**
**3 medium red onions (peeled**
**without breaking the base**
**and quartered)**
**1 large courgette**
**1 small aubergine**
**4 fresh tomatoes**
**Small bunch of fresh basil**
**1 tbsp caster sugar**
**olive oil**
**250g couscous**
**200ml natural yoghurt**
**salt and pepper**

Chop all vegetables to about 1" (2.5cm) cubes.

Chop the basil roughly. Toss all the vegetables with seasoning, the sugar and a good coating of olive oil.

Spread on a roasting pan and put in a pre heated oven (200°C). Roast for 10 minutes, take out and turn the vegetables. Return the tray to the oven and cook for a further 10 minutes.

Meanwhile, prepare the couscous pour it into a measuring jug and note the volume. Put the couscous in a large bowl and toss it with a little salt and a couple of tablespoons of olive oil. Measure the same volume of boiling water in the measuring jug as the couscous. Pour the boiling water over the couscous and stir. Set aside and let it stand until it absorbs the water and cools.

Pack the cooked vegetables into an oven proof dish.

Using your fingers break the couscous into grains. Mix in the yoghurt. Pack this on top of the vegetables.

Bake in a medium oven for 20 to 30 minutes until piping hot and with a light crust on top. Serve immediately.

DEDICATED TO: O'MEARA'S SUPERVALU, PORTUMNA
NOMINATED LOCAL CHARITY: ST DYMPNA'S SCHOOL

# Caitlín Ní Ghiobúin's Eli's Spinach lasagne

This recipe has travelled all over the world and was given to me in Exeter during the last century. A great way to get the kids to eat veg too!

Serves: 4 - 6
Preparation time: 20 minutes
Cooking time: 1 hour approx

**1 tbsp olive oil**
**6 oz lasagne sheets**
**8 oz grated cheddar cheese**
**12 oz fresh or frozen spinach**
**2 tins chopped tomatoes – partly drained**
**1 carton ricotta cheese**
**1 large egg**
**1 tsp each of dried basil, rosemary,oregano (use more if herbs are fresh)**
**1 tsp caraway – roasted**
**2 tbsp chopped parsley**
**(a little brown sugar added to tomatoes if they taste bitter)**
**A 9x9 2 ins deep dish**

Pre heat oven 400°F / 200° C / Gas mark 5

Heat olive oil in medium saucepan and add tomatoes, sugar and herbs. Simmer until liquid is reduced (20 minutes)

Wash fresh spinach and steam for 5 minutes in steamer. Drain well and chop well. (If using frozen Spinach follow instructions on packet)

Lightly whisk egg. Add ricotta cheese, parsley and caraway and gently fold on the cooked spinach

Place ingredients in dish as follows:
a) Half of tomato mixture
b) Layer of lasagne sheets
c) All of spinach mixture
d) Another layer of lasagne sheets
e) Remainder of tomato mixture

Sprinkle grated cheddar cheese on top

Cover dish with greaseproof paper

Bake for 40 minutes

Serve with side salad and rice

# Barbara O'Conchuir's Tomato, Spinach and Feta Quiche

The original recipe comes from a vegetarian cook book I've had for twenty years! Since then I've adapted it to give it a more contemporary flavour.

Serves: 10
Preparation time: 30 minutes (+ 30 minutes chilling time)
Cooking time: 45 minutes

**Pastry:**
**180g flour**
**½ tsp salt**
**125g butter**
**80ml cold water**

**Filling:**
**1 cup cooked spinach**
**½ cup chopped feta cheese**
**½ cup chopped sun dried tomatoes**
**200g cheese (Swiss or similar for a strong taste, mozzarella or similar for a milder taste)**
**25g parmesan cheese**
**1 tbsp plain flour**
**4 eggs**
**430ml rich milk or cream**
**salt and pepper**

To make the pastry: Mix together flour and salt. Cut butter into the flour and mix using your fingers until the mixture resembles oatmeal.

Add ⅔ of the cold water and mix pastry together. Add the remaining water gradually until the mixture comes together but don't allow it to become too soggy.

Shape into a ball, wrap in parchment and refrigerate for 30 minutes.

Remove from parchment, roll out and line a 25-30cm quiche dish. Set aside in the fridge until needed.

Squeeze as much liquid as possible out of the spinach, then chop finely and mix with the feta cheese and sun dried tomatoes.

Grate the cheeses and mix with the flour.

Beat the eggs and milk, add salt and black pepper as required.

Spread spinach, cheese and tomato mix onto pastry in the quiche dish.

Scatter cheese evenly on top.

Pour egg mixture over evenly.

Bake in an oven preheated to 400°F/ 200°C/ Gas 6 for 15 minutes. Reduce temperature to 350 F/ 180°C/ Gas 4 and continue to bake for 30 minutes

The quiche is cooked when a knife is inserted and comes out clean

TOP TIP
Bite size quiches can be made by lining small tart cases with pastry, and baking for 12-15 minutes

FITZPATRICK'S SUPERVALU, ENNISTYMON
NOMINATED LOCAL CHARITY: FRIENDS OF ENNISTYMON HOSPITAL

# Joan Cahill's Herby Chickpea and Nut Loaf

This vegetarian dish is delicious and versatile. It can be served cold, sliced with a salad, or made into burgers by frying in butter and serving with pitta bread. Tasty!

Serves: 6 - 8
Preparation time: 15 - 20 minutes
Cooking time: 35-40 minutes

**1 cup cashew nuts**
**1 cup almonds**
**2 cans chickpeas**
**1 cup cooked brown rice**
**1 handful each of fresh sage, thyme, parsley and rosemary**
**1 egg**
**Juice of ½ lemon**

Finely chop the almonds and cashews in a food processor

Add the chickpeas, rice and finely chopped herbs

Add the lemon juice and the egg

Blend in the food processor until smooth. Season with salt and pepper

Bake in a 1lb loaf tin for 35 minutes at 220°C/425° F/Gas 7

Leave to cool and serve with a colourful salad

KAVANAGH'S SUPERVALU, THOMASTOWN
NOMINATED LOCAL CHARITY: THE AISLING GROUP

# Keefsa Dillon's Potato Rissoles

This recipe is a favourite of my husband's, passed on by my mother in law

Preparation time: 45 minutes
Cooking time: 5 minutes

**200g breadcrumbs**
**400g potatoes (not floury potatoes)**
**1 egg**
**Sprig of fresh thyme**
**Sprig of fresh parsley**
**Salt and pepper**

Cook potatoes and mash well

Mix the mashed potatoes with the breadcrumbs (leaving enough to coat them), herbs and seasoning

Shape the mixture into small cakes

Beat the egg and dip the cakes into the egg, then coat in the remaining breadcrumbs

Deep fry these until golden

TOP TIP
Rissoles vary quite a bit from place to place, some breadcrumbed, others battered and deep fried. They can also have a selection of really tasty fillings that you can add, like vintage cheddar and smokey bacon to jazz up the regular recipe

QUEALLY'S SUPERVALU, KILRUSH
NOMINATED LOCAL CHARITY: WEST CLARE CANCER
GROUP

# Tracy Ann Hood's Broccoli and Mushroom Lasagne

This lasagne is a veggie favourite in our house – even my 3 year old likes it!

Serves: 2 - 3
Preparation time: 30 minutes
Cooking time: 45 minutes

**8 oz broccoli**
**3 oz mushrooms**
**5 oz grated cheddar cheese**
**1½ oz butter**
**1½ oz plain flour**
**1 pint of milk**
**3-4 sheets easi-cook lasagne**
**1 tomato**

Cut broccoli into small florets, place in a pan of cold water. Bring to the boil. Remove from heat drain off the water and leave to one side

Meanwhile slice mushrooms and fry until golden brown. Grate cheese

Melt butter in a saucepan and stir in the flour (taking it away from the heat)

Add the milk gradually, then return to the heat and bring to the boil, whisking continuously
When thickened, stir in 4oz of cheese and allow to melt in the pan

Put half of the broccoli and mushrooms into the bottom of a loaf tin or a small lasagne dish and cover with ⅓ of the sauce. Cover with lasagne pieces

Repeat using the other half of broccoli and mushrooms and another ⅓ of the sauce. Cover with lasagne pieces

Put the last ⅓ of sauce on top, sprinkle with the remaining cheese and garnish with slices of tomato

Cook for approx 45 minutes in a moderate to hot oven (approx 180°, checking regularly

CAHALAN'S SUPERVALU, ABBEYLEIX
NOMINATED LOCAL CHARITY: ABBEYLEIX DISTRICT
HOSPITAL

# Catriona Casey's Low Carb Veggie Shepherd's Pie

This is a delicious vegetarian shepherd's pie, which also uses carrot/turnip and parsnip mash as a low carb alternative

Serves: 4
Preparation time: 30 minutes
Cooking time: 25 minutes

**1 pack of quorn mince**
**1 onion, chopped**
**1 tsp garlic salt**
**6 chopped mushrooms**
**1 cup water (approx)**
**1 cup frozen mixed veg chopped small**
**2 stock cubes**
**1 tbsp tomato ketchup**
**2 tbsp Worchester sauce**
**1 tsp sugar**
**1 tsp mixed herbs**
**2-3 tbsp gravy granules to taste (Bisto or vegetarian alternative)**
**2 large carrots, chopped**
**½ large turnip, chopped**
**1 parsnip, chopped**
**1 tsp olive oil**
**1 tsp butter (optional)**
**Salt and pepper**

Boil the carrot, parsnip and turnip in a saucepan until soft

Meanwhile, fry the chopped onion and mushrooms in oil. Add the quorn mince and cup of frozen mixed vegetables. Stir and add water to prevent drying out

Add stock cubes, garlic and herbs

When the vegetables and mince are almost cooked add the gravy, ketchup, sugar and Worchester sauce and stir well

When the mince is cooked pour the mixture into a small baking tin or lasagne dish

When the carrots, turnip and parsnip are cooked, drain and mash well with butter, salt and pepper

Spoon the veg mash onto the mince and cook in a preheated oven  at 350°F/ 180°C/ Gas 4 until it goes crispy on top

Serve in the same way you would traditional Shepherd's Pie!

DALY'S SUPERVALU, KILLARNEY
NOMINATED LOCAL CHARITY: MS SOCIETY KILLARNEY

# Clodagh McKenna's Gratin Dauphinois

A favourite of the French king's son. This dish is so simple to prepare and so luxurious to eat! This dish can be transformed by just sprinkling some Durrus or Gubbeen Cheese over the top!

Serves 4
Preparation time: 15 minutes
Cooking time: 1 hour 45 minutes

**butter (for greasing dish)**
**1 clove of garlic, crushed**
**6 potatoes**
**1 pint of creamy milk (half cream/milk)**
**salt and pepper**

Grease a roasting dish (6in x 6in approx.) with butter and sprinkle the crushed garlic on the bottom of the dish.

Thinly slice the potatoes and make layers in the dish, seasoning each layer.

Pour the creamy milk over the potatoes and with your hand push down the potatoes until they are completely immersed in the creamy milk.

Cover with a butter wrapper.

Place in a pre-heated oven at 170°C for1½ hours and then remove the butter wrapper and turn up the heat to 200°C until the top is golden.

DEDICATED TO: PETTITT'S SUPERVALU, WEXFORD
NOMINATED LOCAL CHARITY: FRIENDS OF WEXFORD
GENERAL HOSPITAL

# Clodagh McKenna's Spring Potato Salad

I love eating this potato salad with a bbq or with poached fish on a warm spring day!

Serves: 4 as an accompaniment
Preparation time: 10 minutes
Cooking time (potatoes) 25 minutes

**800g new potatoes, cooked**
**200g crème fraîche**
**4 spring onions, sliced**
**1 lemon, zest and juice**
**salt and pepper**

Cut the potatoes in half.

While they are still warm add the crème fraîche, sliced spring onions, lemon zest and juice and season with salt and pepper.

Stir gently and leave to cool.

Serve as part of a salad or as an accompaniment to your favourite dish

DEDICATED TO: BAGNALL'S SUPERVALU, KINNEGAD
NOMINATED LOCAL CHARITY: SAPLINGS AUTISTIC
SCHOOL, MULLINGAR

# Mary Cunningham's Ratatouille

I first cooked this dish as a Sunday treat and everyone enjoyed it so much that we eat it regularly now! It's also a great way of providing the daily intake of vegetables!

Serves: 4
Preparation time: 15
Cooking time: 45 minutes

**1 red pepper, deseeded**
**2 yellow peppers, deseeded**
**2 courgettes**
**1 aubergine**
**4 plum tomatoes**
**2 red onions**
**8 basil leaves roughly torn**
**1 tsp coriander seeds, crushed**
**3 tbsp extra virgin olive oil**
**3 cloves garlic, crushed**
**3 tbsp white wine**
**Salt and freshly ground black pepper**

Preheat oven to 350°F/ 180°C/ Gas 4

Slice aubergine, sprinkle with salt and leave in a colander for 30 minutes. Pat dry and place in an oven proof dish

Chop peppers into bite size pieces and season with salt and pepper

Slice courgette and season with salt and pepper

Cut tomatoes into quarters and season

Cut red onions into quarters

Add all the above to the oven proof dish

Tear basil leaves and toss crushed garlic and coriander seeds into the vegetables with a metal spoon

Pour white wine over the vegetables

Pour olive oil over the vegetables, toss then place in the oven and bake for 45 minutes until the vegetables are tender. Serve immediately

FLEMING'S SUPERVALU, ROSCOMMON
NOMINATED LOCAL CHARITY: ROSCOMMON BROTHERS OF CHARITY SERVICES

# Stephanie Mangan's Sundried Tomato & Spinach Tartlets

These irresistible individual tartlets combine all my favourite ingredients and never fail to impress!

Serves: 6
Preparation time: 15 minutes
Cooking time: 20 minutes

**1 pack of ready to roll puff pastry**
**2 eggs**
**100ml milk**
**1 handful chopped spinach**
**Some parmesan shavings**
**2 tbsp sun dried tomatoes, chopped**
**Salt and Pepper**

Cut pastry into 12 rounds

Place these into a bun tray and bake in a preheated oven at 180°C for 8 minutes

Mix the milk with the eggs and add salt and pepper to taste

Place spinach and sundried tomatoes in each pastry case and pour the egg mixture over them

Bake in a moderate oven for approx 20 minutes

Serve garnished with parmesan shavings and a rocket salad

CADDEN'S SUPERVALU, OLDCASTLE
NOMINATED LOCAL CHARITY: THE AISLING GROUP

# Chef Phelim Byrne's Savoury Spring Onion Pancakes

Makes about 16 mini pancakes
Preparation time: 5 minutes
Cooking time: 5 minutes

**1 cup plain flour**
**2 spring onions, chopped**
**300 ml buttermilk**
**1 egg**
**Salt and pepper**

Simply place these ingredients into a bowl and whisk together to achieve a smooth thick batter.

Season well with salt and pepper.

Pour 2 tbsp of cooking oil into a preheated frying pan.

Drop dsrt spoons of the mix into the pan 4 at a time to achieve little individual pancakes.

Cook on a low heat for about a minute or until golden on the other side.

Now gently turn over and allow to cook through on a low heat. The pancakes will be light and fluffy at this stage.

Remove from the pan and top with a teaspoon of crème fraîche. Then choose your preferred topping a little rosette of smoked salmon or a sliver of cured meats are also delicious.

For a vegetarian option top this with some diced and roasted Mediterranean vegetables cooked in olive oil and sea salt for a tasty snack.

Enjoy!

Tip:
Make the pancake batter up to a day in advance and keep in the fridge for further use, the sweet variety are the same with no salt and pepper or spring onion, just lashings of maple syrup

DEDICATED TO: BUCKLEY'S SUPERVALU, MULLINGAR
NOMINATED LOCAL CHARITY: SR. FINBAR'S COMMUNITY CENTRE

# Margaret O'Connor's Pear and Parsnip Soup

I added ginger and pears to this basic vegetable soup to transform it and give it a lovely Oriental taste. We love it!

Serves: 6
Preparation time: 15 minutes
Cooking time: 30 minutes

**1 medium onion, chopped**
**1 large potato, chopped**
**2 cloves of garlic, crushed**
**1 tsp grated root ginger**
**1 oz butter**
**2 pears, peeled**
**4 sticks celery, chopped**
**1½ pints chicken stock**
**2 parsnips**
**Fresh black pepper**

Sauté the onion and garlic in some butter

Add celery, parsnips, potato and ginger and sweat for 10 minutes

Add chicken stock (made with 2 stock cubes)

Slice pear and add to the pan. Season with black pepper

Simmer for 20 minutes

Allow to cool, then blend until smooth

Serve with buttered crusty bread for a winter warming lunch or as a starter

CAHILL'S SUPERVALU, BALLYBUNION
NOMINATED LOCAL CHARITY: LOCAL TIDY TOWNS

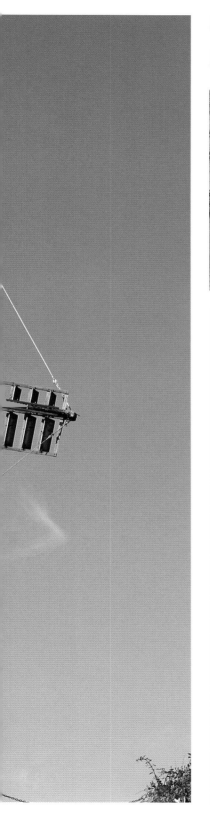

# Baking and treats

Recipes

# Chef Hugh McNally's Sundried Tomato Bread

Try serving this Italian style bread at your next BBQ – it's sure to get your guests talking!

Makes 1 loaf
Preparation time: 15 minutes plus 1 hour proving time
Cooking time: 30 minutes

**550g strong white flour**
**1 tsp sea salt**
**7g sachet dried yeast**
**1 tsp caster sugar**
**1 tbsp finely chopped fresh rosemary and thyme**
**8 sun dried tomatoes, roughly chopped**
**1 tbsp tomato purée**
**1 pint tepid water**
**1 tsp olive oil**
**salt and pepper**

Sieve the flour and salt into a bowl and add the dried yeast and sugar.

Add the herbs, sundried tomatoes and tomato purée and season with salt and pepper.

Make a well in the centre of the mixture and pour in the water.

Mix all these ingredients into a soft dough. Turn onto a floured surface and knead for approximately 5 minutes until smooth and elastic.

Then place the dough into a bowl and cover with cling film to allow the yeast to work. Leave in a warm area to prove for about 1 hour.

When the dough has almost doubled in size remove it from the bowl, shape into a long sausage shape about 10 inches long x 3 inches wide and place on an oiled baking tray.

Brush the bread with the oil and place in a preheated oven for approximately 30 minutes at 200°C until golden.

DEDICATED TO: HORKAN'S SUPERVALU, TEMPLEOGUE
NOMINATED LOCAL CHARITY: ST. MICHAEL'S HOUSE

# Kathleen Reidy's Bacon, Onion and Herb Scones

An elderly neighbour who had a large family gave me this recipe. They loved it and now my family love it too!

Serves: 4
Preparation time: 15 minutes
Cooking time: 25 minutes

**1lb self raising flour**
**2-3 oz margarine**
**1 egg**
**6 oz streaky bacon, diced**
**1 onion, chopped**
**1 tsp mixed herbs**
**200ml little milk**

Fry the onion and diced bacon together.

Sieve the flour into a mixing bowl and add the herbs. Rub the margarine into the flour.

Next, add the egg, milk, onion and bacon and mix to a soft dough.

Knead on a floured board.

Cut the dough into squares and placed on a baking tray.

Bake at 400° F/ 200°C/ Gas 6 for 25 minutes.

GARVEY'S SUPERVALU, CASTLEISLAND
NOMINATED LOCAL CHARITY: CASTLEISLAND BRANCH OF
THE KERRY HOSPICE

# Kathleen Bolger's Striped Bread

I have never seen this recipe elsewhere – it's of Northern origin passed on by word of mouth by my Gran

Serves: 6-8
Preparation time: 20 minutes
Cooking time: 30 - 35 minutes

**2 lb flour**
**2 tsp of salt**
**1 tsp of bicarbonate of soda**
**2 oz butter**
**1 pint of buttermilk**
**1 tbsp treacle**

Sift all the dry ingredients together. Rub in the butter

Add buttermilk and mix to form a soft dough

Remove 1/3 of the mixture and place in a bowl. Add the treacle and mix well

Divide the white bread in half and knead all 3 portions

Shape into 1 inch rounds and sandwich the dark treacle bread between the two white soda breads

Press firmly together

Place on a floured baking sheet, cut a cross on top

Bake in a preheated oven at 425°F/ 220°C/ Gas 7 for 30-35 minutes

PETTITT'S SUPERVALU, ENNISCORTHY
NOMINATED LOCAL CHARITY: SAINT VINCENT DE PAUL ENNISCORTHY

# Maureen Hannon's Healthy Brown Bread

This is a family favourite of ours, passed on from one of my cousins

Makes: 2 loaves
Preparation time: 20 minutes
Cooking time: 45 minutes

**1½ lbs spelt flour**
**4 heaped dsp each; pumpkin seeds, sesame seeds, sunflower seeds, bran, wheatgerm, and pinhead oatmeal**
**2 large eggs or 3 small eggs**
**1 small tub of yoplait plain yoghurt**
**¾ pt milk approx**
**1 heaped tsp bread soda**
**3 heaped tsp baking powderr**

Mix all the dry ingredients together

In a separate bowl, beat the eggs. Add the yogurt and mix well

Add milk to the eggs and yogurt and then mix, add the result to the mixture of dry ingredients- it should be fairly wet

Put in 2 greased loaf tins

Bake at 180°C for 45 minutes in a fan oven/ 200°C in an ordinary oven

Turn tins after 25 minutes

RYAN'S SUPERVALU, TOGHER
NOMINATED LOCAL CHARITY: TIR NA N'ÓG RESPITE SERVICES

# Patrick Doherty's Monkey Bread

Yummy and scrummy when it's in my tummy!

Makes 1 loaf
Preparation time: 20 - 30 minutes
Cooking time: 1 hour

**4 oz butter**
**8 oz self raising flour**
**3 oz brown sugar**
**2 oz raisins**
**2 eggs**
**3 tbsp honey**
**4 ripe bananas**

Rub the butter and flour together in a large mixing bowl

Add the sugar and raisins

Add the eggs and the honey and mix well

Mash the bananas in a separate bowl, and then add to the mixture

Give it a good stir for a few minutes

Grease a loaf tin and pour in the mixture

Bake in a preheated oven at 350° F/ 180° C/ Gas 4 for about 1 hour

DAVIS' SUPERVALU, LONGFORD
NOMINATED LOCAL CHARITY: LONGFORD HOSPICE

# Sarah Jayne Holden's Magic Mix Cakes

Nan's famous sandwich cakes which never flopped or cracked. An old magic mix with a new fresh and fruity filling!

Serves: 10
Preparation time: 20 minutes
Cooking time: 35 minutes

**Cake:**
**6 oz self raising flour**
**1 tsp baking powder**
**pinch of salt**
**6 oz butter**
**6 oz caster sugar**
**3 medium eggs**
**½ tsp vanilla essence**
**2 tbsp milk if needed**

**Filling:**
**2 x 200g tubs of low fat cream cheese**
**6 heaped tbsp icing sugar**
**zest and Juice of 1 lime (or enough to make a paste)**
**400g fresh sliced strawberries**
**3 tbsp SuperValu Supreme strawberry conserve – slightly warmed**

For the Cake:
Mix together the flour, baking powder and salt. In a separate bowl, combine the butter and sugar and beat until creamed together. Add the eggs to the creamed mixture one at a time. Stir the vanilla essence through. Finally add the dry ingredients, mixing to combine well (add a little milk if the mixture is too dry).

Beat all of the cake ingredients together until light and fluffy.

Divide the mixture evenly into 2 greased and lined 20.5cm (8") sandwich cake tins.

Bake in a preheated oven at 375°F/ 190°C/ Gas 5 for 35 minutes.

Check if cooked by pressing a skewer into the centre – it's cooked if it comes out clean.

Leave to cool. Meanwhile, mix together the cream cheese, icing sugar and zest and juice of lime – adding enough juice to give you a paste.

Spread the paste on one side of the first cake and add the chopped strawberries.

Spread the jam on the underside of the other cake, and sandwich both together.

Cut into generous wedges and serve.

MINIHANE'S SUPERVALU, GORT
NOMINATED LOCAL CHARITY: SOUTH GALWAY SOCIAL SERVICES

# Frances McDonagh's Apple and Sugar Crunch Cakes

This was a totally experimental recipe by my mother – and the result was scrumptious buns which are impossible to resist!

Makes: 18 buns
Preparation time: 10-15 minutes
Cooking time: 20 minutes

**6 oz self raising flour**
**2 eggs**
**5 oz chopped cooking apple**
**4 oz margarine**
**4 oz castor sugar**
**1 tbsp milk**
**1½ tsp baking powder**
**½ tsp nutmeg**
**½ tsp cinnamon**

Cream together the sugar and margarine

Into a separate bowl sieve the flour, baking powder and spices

Add the prepared flour into the creamed mixture and fold together

Beat the eggs, and add to the mixture. Mix thoroughly

Add the chopped apple and milk and mix well

Spoon the mixture into bun cases and bake on a baking tray in a preheated oven at 220°C/425° F/Gas 7 for 15-20 minutes

KANE AND MCCARTNEY'S SUPERVALU, KILLESTER
NOMINATED LOCAL CHARITY: CENTRAL REMEDIAL CLINIC
CLONTARF

# Myrika Nic Dhonnachá's Mum's Munchies

When my mom was young, her mother used to make these cookies for their school lunches. Then, when she first left home she got really home sick and getting these cookies in a package from her mom one day really helped, Now I help make them and bring them to school.

Makes 30-36 cookies
Preparation time: 5 - 10 minutes
Cooking time: 18 - 22 minutes

**2 cups rolled oats**
**½ cup of sugar**
**½ cup flour**
**½ cup of sultanas (optional)**
**1 tablespoon golden syrup**
**2 teaspoons bicarbonate of soda**
**2 tablespoons boiling water**
**½ cup butter melted**

Preheat oven to 160°C

Mix the dry ingredients together in a bowl

Mix the butter, water and golden syrup together. Then add the bicarbonate of soda to the mixture. While this is still frothing pour this into the dry ingredients and mix thoroughly

Drop spoonfuls onto a tray allowing space for the mixture to spread

Bake in the preheated oven for about 18-22 minutes (until golden brown)

Allow to cool and enjoy

CLARKE'S SUPERVALU, BARNA
NOMINATED LOCAL CHARITY: SPECIAL OLYMPICS

# Josephine Allen's Bill's Brownies

My 6 year old son loves cooking with me, and this is his favourite recipe!

Serves: 8 -12
Preparation time: 15 minutes
Cooking time: 30 minutes

**225g butter, diced**
**225g good quality chocolate, chopped**
**4 eggs**
**225g caster sugar**
**110g plain flour**
**Icing sugar for dusting**

Melt butter and chocolate in a heat proof dish over boiling water.

Whisk the eggs and the sugar for about 10 minutes.

Fold in the melted chocolate and sieve in the flour to the eggs and sugar.

Pour the mixture into a tray of size approx 33 x 22cm.

Cook in a preheated oven at 160° for about 30 minutes.

Remove from the oven, cover with a damp towel and allow to cool.

Dust with icing sugar and cut into squares... yum yum!

SUPERVALU NEWMARKET CO-OP, NEWMARKET
NOMINATED LOCAL CHARITY: ST. JOSEPH'S FOUNDATION
IN CHARLEVILLE

# Una McGarrigle's Chocolate Chip Shortbread

A mouth watering recipe, perfect with a hot cup of tea or coffee!

Makes 16 pieces
Preparation time: 10 minutes
Cooking time: 15 minutes

**½ cup softened butter**
**½ cup sugar**
**1 tsp vanilla essence**
**1 cup flour**
**¼ tsp salt**
**½ cup mini chocolate chips**

Preheat oven to 190°C/375°F/Gas 5

Beat butter and sugar in large bowl until light and fluffy

Next, beat in vanilla essence

Add flour and salt. Beat at a low speed (gently)

Stir in chocolate chips with mixing spoon

Divide the dough in half. Press each half into an ungreased round 8 inch tin

Bake for approx 12 minutes or until the edges are golden brown

Score shortbread with sharp knife taking care not to cut completely through. Make 8 wedges per tin

Let tins stand on wire for 10 minutes. Then invert shortbread onto wire cooling trays, cool completely and break into wedges

Store tightly sealed at room temperature or freeze for up to 3 months

KAVANAGH'S SUPERVALU, DONEGAL
NOMINATED LOCAL CHARITY: DONEGAL HOSPICE,
DONEGAL TOWN

# Lisa McCaul's Chocolate Biscuit Cake

My mum makes this for my birthday, and my friends all love it!

Serves: 10 - 15
Preparation time: 30 minutes
Chilling time: overnight

**4 oz butter**
**1 packet of digestive biscuits**
**1 bar milk or plain chocolate (200g)**
**1 can condensed milk**
**Chocolate for decorating (150g-200g)**

Put the chocolate, condensed milk and butter in a bowl and melt in the microwave or over a pot of boiling water

Break the biscuits into small pieces in a large mixing bowl

Pour the melted mixture over the biscuits, and mix together well

Press into a well greased, lined tin and put in the fridge

Allow to set for a few hours, ideally overnight. Turn out onto a sheet of greaseproof paper

Melt another 150g-200g bar of chocolate and pour over the top and sides of the cake .Allow to set, then serve in large chunks

TOP TIP
A tasty addition to this is to add some sultanas and nuts. Yum!

FOY'S SUPERVALU, COOTEHILL
NOMINATED LOCAL CHARITY: HOLY FAMILY SCHOOL

# Nicola O'Rourke's Orange and Cranberry Bread

This recipe came about by accident. I had intended to make a date and rosemary bread but had neither ingredient... and so cranberry and orange bread was born!

Makes 10 slices
Preparation time: 10-15 minutes plus rising time
Cooking time: 40 minutes

**300 mls warm water**
**1 tbsp olive oil**
**½ tbsp runny honey**
**2 tsp salt**
**125g cranberries (fresh, frozen or dried)**
**1 orange (washed)**
**450g strong brown bread flour with malted wheatgrain**
**1½ tsp fast action yeast**

Preheat the oven to 190°C. Put flour, salt, cranberries and zest of orange into a bowl. Sprinkle the yeast over this

Put the water, honey, oil and juice of the orange (including some bits of flesh) into a jug

Combine the liquid into the flour mixture to make a soft dough

Knead dough for about 10 minutes, shape and fit into a prepared 2lb loaf tin. Leave to rise until doubled in size

Glaze with an egg wash and place in preheated oven. Bake until golden brown (Approx 40 minutes)

This loaf is a happy accident! Delicious as part of a rasher sandwich, with salad or just on it's own

KAVANAGH'S SUPERVALU, WESTPORT
NOMINATED LOCAL CHARITY: ST VINCENT DE PAUL

# Maureen O'Flaherty's Savoury Breads

It's easy to adapt a basic white bread recipe to make a large array of savoury breads

Preparation time: 20 minutes
Cooking time: 20 - 25 minutes

**1lb strong white flour**
**4 tablespoons of corn oil**
**1 sachet of dried yeast**
**¾ pint of warm water**
**½ teaspoon sugar**
**Salt and Pepper**
**Variations to add to recipe:**
**Herb Bread: Add 2 tbsp of fresh mixed herbs or**
**3 tbsp of dried mixed herbs and 2 finely chopped**
**garlic cloves**
**Garlic Bread: Add 6 finely chopped garlic cloves**
**and 2 tbsp of parsley**
**Olive Bread: Add 20 stoned, chopped olives**
**Sundried Tomato Bread: Add a small jar of**
**sun dried tomatoes, chopped**

Combine your preferred variation from above (or one of your own!) with flour, yeast, sugar, salt and pepper. Add the oil and some water and mix through

Add more water and mix again, adding enough water to make a sticky dough

Turn dough onto a floured surface and knead for 10 minutes

Divide dough into 2 equal pieces and put into two greased 1lb loaf tins

Brush top of dough lightly with oil

Put each loaf tin in a plastic bag and seal. Put these in a warm place for 30 minutes or until dough has doubled in size (Prove)

Then put bread into a preheated oven 220° C/425° F/Gas 7 for 20-25 minutes

Check bread. If it is lightly browned remove from tin and tap bottom of loaf with fingertips. If it sounds hollow the bread is now cooked

# Chef Domini Kemp's white chocolate, marshmallow & orange Ghosts

Fun rice crispy treats flavoured with orange zest and marshmallows, decorated with raisins or currants, but super-sweet!

Makes 10 squares
Preparation time: 10 minutes
Setting time: a couple of hours, approximately

**50g butter, and extra for greasing**
**200g marshmallows**
**180g rice crispies**
**200g bar white chocolate, chopped**
**peel of one orange**
**handful raisins or currants**

Melt together the butter and marshmallows over a low heat in a large non-stick pan.

Remove from heat, stir in the rice crispies and press into a buttered tin (approximately 18cm/ 7" square) and allow to cool.

Melt the white chocolate in a bowl over boiling water and pour over the rice crispies.

Allow to set, cut into squares and decorate with orange peel and raisins. Cut into squares/shapes when cool.

Top tip

Cut orange peel into all sorts of fun shapes to make smiley or scary Hallowe'en faces.

DEDICATED TO: KANE'S SUPERVALU, TALBOT ST, DUBLIN
NOMINATED LOCAL CHARITY: IRISH CANCER SOCIETY

# Chef Domini Kemp's Pineapple and Strawberry Fruit Skewers

These are light and refreshing, and fun for all to eat!

Serves: 4 - 6
Preparation time: 20 minutes

**Handful of fresh mint leaves**
**2 tablespoons soft brown sugar**
**Juice of two limes**
**1 pineapple, peeled and chopped into chunks**
**1 punnet strawberries, sliced in half**

Roughly chop the mint leaves and add the sugar. If you have a pestle and mortar, this would be handy to use, if not chop by hand or blend in a processor.

Mix in the lime juice and taste.

Add more sugar or lime juice as required, or some water if you would like to make it weaker.

Put the pineapple and strawberries on skewers and serve, dipping into the mint sugar or pouring some of the mint sugar on top.

DEDICATED TO: LEHANE'S SUPERVALU, LIMERICK
NOMINATED LOCAL CHARITY: DOWN SYNDROME IRELAND

# Mairéad McMahon's Portuguese Honey Cake

This recipe has proved a favourite at our book club, eaten while discussing literature. Books and cake – the perfect combination!

Makes: 2 loaves
Preparation time: 10 minutes
Cooking time: 40 minutes

**3 or 4 large eggs**
**2 cups castor sugar**
**3 cups self raising flour**
**1 cup milk**
**1 cup sunflower oil**
**3 tsp cinnamon**
**2 tsp baking powder**
**3 dsp of honey**
**(use a large tea cup to measure)**

Preheat oven to 180°C

Put all ingredients into a bowl and mix very well

Grease two 2lb loaf tins and pour mixture in

Bake for 30-40 minutes in the oven

Enjoy plain, or decorated with melted dark chocolate

As this makes 2 loaves, I usually freeze one of them

FLYNN'S SUPERVALU, BANAGHER
NOMINATED LOCAL CHARITY: SPECIAL OLYMPICS

# Marian McCormack's Rhubarb and Yoghurt Cake

This is a beautiful, moist, easy to make cake. It's always a favourite with everyone who tastes it

Serves: 8
Preparation time: 10 minutes
Cooking time: 1 hour

**150g finely sliced fresh rhubarb**
**310g self raising flour, sifted**
**250g castor sugar**
**125g plain yoghurt**
**1 tsp vanilla essence**
**1 tsp rosewater**
**2 eggs, lightly beaten**
**125g unsalted butter, melted**

Preheat the oven to 350°F/180°C/Gas 4

Lightly grease a 23cm round cake tin and line base with baking paper

Combine rhubarb, flour and sugar in a bowl

Add vanilla essence, eggs, yoghurt, rosewater and melted butter, stirring until mixture is just combined

Spoon mixture into cake tin and bake in the preheated oven for 1 hour, or until a skewer comes out clean when inserted into the centre of the cake

Slice into generous wedges and serve

CAHILL'S SUPERVALU, CASTLEREA
NOMINATED LOCAL CHARITY: ST MICHAEL'S SPECIAL SCHOOL

# Margaret Winser-Grainger's Grandma Lindsley's Gingerbread

This recipe has been passed down for five generations. As children it was a really special treat which we loved!

Makes 8 - 10 pieces
Preparation time: 15 minutes
Cooking time: 20 - 25 minutes

**2 cups of self raising flour**
**1½ tsp ground ginger (or to taste)**
**3 tbsp caster sugar**
**¼ lb butter or margarine, diced**
**1 cup of boiling water**
**3 tbsp black treacle**
**1 tsp baking soda**

Mix together flour, ginger and sugar, then rub in the butter or margarine and make a well in the centre.

In a saucepan combine the boiling water and treacle and bring to the boil. When it is boiling add the baking soda (Note: This will froth) and stir.

Pour this into the well made in the flour mixture and mix well.

Line a large baking tin and pour mixture into it.

Bake in a moderate oven (approx 180°C) for 20-25 minutes.

(Note: Ovens differ so cooking time may vary)

BROOKES' SUPERVALU, YOUGHAL
NOMINATED LOCAL CHARITY: YOUGHAL COMMUNITY HOSPITAL

# Rose Byrne's Rose's Pear and Apple Tart

I made this tart by accident a while ago. I did not have enough apples for the tart but had some pears in the fruit bowl hence the pear and apple tart - Delicious, everyone loves it!!

Serves: 8
Preparation time: 15 minutes
Cooking time: 20-25 minutes

**8 oz plain flour, and extra for dusting**
**pinch of salt**
**4 oz margarine**
**drop of water**
**2 large cooking apples (peeled and sliced)**
**1 oz caster sugar**
**½ teaspoon ground cloves**
**2 large pears (peeled and sliced)**

To make pastry, sieve flour and add salt. Rub in the margarine (until resembles breadcrumbs).

Add enough water to bind together. Turn onto a table dusted with flour. Knead and divide pastry in two. Roll out two large circles.

Line an oven proof tart plate with one pastry disc and add apples and pears. Sprinkle ground cloves and sugar over the top. Wet around the edges.

Place the remaining pastry on top and press all round.

Bake at 180°C fan oven for approx 25 minutes.

Serve with cream or ice cream.

HICKSON'S SUPERVALU, TULLOW
NOMINATED LOCAL CHARITY: CARLOW/ KILKENNY
HOME CARE TEAM

# Maire Mhic Aodha's Norwegian Apple Cake

This cake is quick and easy to make and is a favourite in our house
25
Serves: 8-10
Preparation time: 15 minutes
Cooking time: 15 minutes

**2 large eggs**
**9 oz caster sugar**
**4 oz butter, and extra for greasing**
**Generous quarter pint of milk**
**6½ oz plain flour, and extra for dusting**
**3 teaspoons baking powder**
**3-4 cooking apples**

Grease and flour an 8 x 12 inch roasting tin.

Whisk the eggs and 8 oz of the sugar until the mixture is thick and creamy, and the whisk leaves a trail when it is lifted out. (Using an electric or hand whisk is easier, and cuts down on washing up!).

Put the butter and milk into a pan. Bring to the boil and immediately stir into the eggs and sugar.

Sieve in the flour and baking powder so that there are no lumps of flour, and fold carefully into the batter until smooth.

Pour the mixture into the prepared roasting tin. Peel, core and slice the apples, arrange them over the batter.

Bake in moderately hot oven 200°C for about 25 minutes.
Allow to cool in the tin, then turn out and serve generous slices.

NESTOR'S SUPERVALU, ORANMORE
NOMINATED LOCAL CHARITY: GALWAY HOSPICE

# Philomena Calnan's Family Cake

My mum used to make us a family cake once a week if we were good. It's a lovely soft cake that was worth waiting for

Makes 8 slices
Preparation time: 30 minutes
Cooking time: 2 hours

**1lb cream flour**
**8 oz sugar**
**8 oz margarine**
**8 oz currants, sultanas and mixed peel**
**2 oz chopped almonds**
**Rind of 2 large lemons**
**4 eggs**
**¼ pint of milk**

Cream the margarine and sugar, beat in the eggs

Mix the fruit, almonds and lemon rind together

Add this to the creamed mixture gradually, alternating with the sifted flour

Stir well but do not beat

Add enough milk to make a stiff dropping consistency, mixing well

Pour the mixture into a prepared cake tin, spread it evenly allowing for a slight hollow in the centre

Bake in a preheated oven for approx 2 hours at 180°C

BIGGS' SUPERVALU, BANTRY
NOMINATED LOCAL CHARITY: BANTRY CARE FOR THE AGED

# Mary Foley's Granny's Guinness Cake

My granny taught me to make this cake and I've added my own ingredients to make it richer. I've been making this cake for 20 years!

Makes: 10-20 slices
Preparation time: 20-25 minutes (plus overnight soaking/cooling)
Cooking time: 1½ hours

**1 small bottle of Guinness**
**12 oz raisins**
**8 oz sultanas**
**4 oz mixed peel**
**8 oz margarine or butter**
**8 oz Demerara sugar**
**10 oz plain flour**
**4 eggs**
**Orange rind and juice**
**½ tsp baking powder**
**Spices to flavour – cinnamon/spice**

Place all fruit and Guinness in a bowl and leave overnight

Cream margarine and sugar. Add eggs and flour and mix well

Add all the fruit and baking powder and mix again

Turn the mixture into a 9" cake tin and bake in a preheated oven at 150°C for 1½ hours approx

Leave to cool in the tin overnight

Cut into wedges and enjoy!

CAULFIELD'S SUPERVALU, THE QUAY, NEW ROSS
NOMINATED LOCAL CHARITY: CBS PRIMARY SCHOOL

# Maria Fullerton's Caramel Squares

No counting calories, we just enjoy every last crumb!

Serves: 10
Preparation time: 15 minutes + cooling time
Cooking time: 15 minutes

**4 oz margarine**
**2 oz caster sugar**
**6 oz plain flour**
**1 x 200g chocolate, chopped**

**Caramel**
**4 oz butter**
**4 oz caster sugar**
**½ tin condensed milk**
**1 tbsp golden syrup**

Beat margarine and sugar together. Beat in flour. Place in tray in a preheated oven 180°C/ 350°F/ Gas mark 4 and bake till golden brown (approximately 15 minutes). Allow to cool.

To make the caramel heat the butter, sugar, condensed milk and golden syrup until golden brown. Spread evenly on the cool biscuit base. Allow to cool.

Meanwhile melt chocolate in a bowl set over a pan of simmering water.

Spread melted chocolate over caramel and allow to cool. The caramel squares should ideally be placed in the fridge to set.

KAVANAGH'S SUPERVALU, BUNCRANA
NOMINATED LOCAL CHARITY: CASH NA COR RESOURCE CENTRE

# Mary Moloney's Healthy Muffins

This is an old recipe, changed to my own taste. You can add more apple if you wish to make them extra moist!

Makes 30 muffins
Preparation time: 20 minutes
Cooking time: 30 minutes

**8 oz plain flour**
**6 oz brown flour**
**6 oz caster sugar**
**2 tsp baking powder**
**2 tsp cinnamon**
**6 oz carrot, grated**
**1 cooking apple, grated**
**2 oz walnuts, chopped**
**3 oz raisins**
**2 oz desiccated coconut**
**3 eggs**
**200 ml sunflower oil**

Mix both flours, caster sugar, baking powder and cinnamon together in a large bowl.

Stir in the grated carrot, apple, nuts, raisins and coconut.

Stir in the eggs and oil.

Place about 30 bun cases on a baking tray and spoon out the mixture.

Bake in a preheated oven at 150°C for approximately 30 minutes.

CONNOLLY'S SUPERVALU, BAGENALSTOWN
NOMINATED LOCAL CHARITY: CARLOW/KILKENNY HOME CARE TEAM

# Betty Gowen's Fruity Wholemeal Bread with Caraway Seeds

This was one of my Granny's favourite breads which I still always enjoy. It's delicious whether for breakfast, school lunches or supper!

Serves: 4 - 5
Preparation time: 6 minutes
Cooking time: 35 minutes

**½ lb strong white flour**
**½ lb wholemeal flour**
**1 level tsp of bread soda**
**2 level tsp Bex tartar**
**½ tsp salt**
**2 oz sugar**
**4 oz raisins or sultanas**
**2 tsp caraway seeds**
**½ - ¾ pint buttermilk or sour milk**
**1 egg**

Preheat oven to 220°C

Sift flour, salt and raising agents together

Add wholemeal flour, dried fruit, sugar and caraway seeds

Beat the egg and add to the milk. Mix this gradually into the dry ingredients to form a soft dough

Knead lightly, shape into a round cake and place on a lightly floured baking tray

Mark the top with a cross and sprinkle with some caraway seeds

Bake for approx 35 minutes. When cooked remove from the oven and cool on a wire tray

Delicious served warm with a smear of butter

RIORDAN'S SUPERVALU, FERMOY
NOMINATED LOCAL CHARITY: COPE FOUNDATION, FERMOY

# Nessa Whelan's Tea Brack

My grandmother always had a tea brack ready for our visit and served it with a generous serving of butter. Just gorgeous!

Serves: 10
Preparation time: 20 minutes + soaking overnight
Cooking time: 1 - 1¼ hour

**12 fl oz cold tea**
**7 oz soft brown sugar**
**12 oz mixed dried fruit**
**1 oz unsalted butter**
**10 oz self raising flour**
**1 egg, beaten**

Put tea, sugar and dried fruit in a bowl and cover overnight. (Tea that has been left over during the day can be saved and used).

The next day, well grease an 8" round tin or 2 x 1lb loaf tins.

Mix the flour and egg into the soaked ingredients to make a smooth mixture.

Pour into the tin and bake in a moderate oven pre-heated to 325°F/ 170°C/ Gas 3 for about 1¼ hours. The tea brack is ready if a knife put into the brack comes out clean.

Turn out and cool on a wire tray and serve with lashings of butter

FLYNN'S SUPERVALU, TURLOUGHMORE
NOMINATED LOCAL CHARITY: ST VINCENT DE PAUL

# Anne Deane's Mars Mallow Delights

This is a simple tray baked treat, a family favourite that doesn't last in our house! It's easy to make and a treat at any time

Serves: 8 plus, depending on how big you cut the slices
Preparation time: 15 minutes

**4 x 54g Mars Bars (Standard size Mars bar)**
**4 oz butter**
**6 oz crushed rich tea biscuits**
**2 oz mini marshmallows, chopped in half**
**2 oz cereal crushed (Fitnesse or Rice Crispies)**
**1 oz washed and dried cherries**
**1 oz chopped almonds (optional)**
**150g chocolate (melted)**

Melt Mars bars and butter together in a glass bowl suspended over a saucepan of simmering water

Stir with a wooden spoon until completely melted

Add all dry ingredients and mix well

When thoroughly mixed, empty the mixture into a Swiss roll tin ( 11"x7" lined with baking parchment) and press down lightly until the tin is all covered

When this is done cover the mixture with melted chocolate and leave in the fridge to set

Slice into squares and keep in the fridge until needed

HEALY'S SUPERVALU, DUNMANWAY
NOMINATED LOCAL CHARITY: DUNMANWAY HOSPITAL

# Deirdre Kelly's Nutty Flap Jacks

These flapjacks are great lunchbox treats!

Makes 10 flapjacks
Preparation time: 10 minutes
Cooking time: 20-25 minutes

**4 oz self raising flour**
**4 oz porridge**
**4 oz castor sugar**
**3 oz coconut**
**1 g bran**
**1 oz nibbed almonds**
**4 oz butter**
**2 tsp golden syrup**

Mix all the dry ingredients together.

Melt syrup and butter together in a pot over a medium heat.

Add the result to the dried ingredients.

Press into a baking tray of size approx 9" x 15".

Bake in a preheated oven at 180°C for 20 minutes.

Slice when hot, allow to cool before serving.

COLCLOUGH'S SUPERVALU, ROSCREA
NOMINATED LOCAL CHARITY: SISTERS OF THE SACRED
HEART OF JESUS AND MARY

# Mary Moynihan's Gingernut Log

I developed this recipe when living in New Zealand after deciding to experiment one night!

Serves: 8
Preparation time: 10 minutes
Chilling time: Overnight

**1 packet of ginger nut biscuits**
**1 flake**
**1 carton of cream**
**1 tin crushed pineapple**
**1-2 drops liquor (Tia Maria or similar)**

Whip cream until thick

Drain juice from pineapple and mix with the cream and the liquor

Place a long piece of tin foil on a flat surface

Open the packet of biscuits onto the foil, and sandwich the mixture between each biscuits

Repeat for the whole pack, then wrap the tin foil around the long roll and refrigerate overnight

Serve on a long dish and decorated with whipped cream and crumbled flake

# Desserts

Recipes

# Clodagh McKenna's Kids' Mini Trifles

This is a great alternative for kids (and adults!) for Christmas as the Christmas pudding can tend to be to heavy for kids. Its also great for the summer using lots of seasonal summer berries.

Makes 6 glasses
Preparation time: 10 minutes
Cooking time: 20 minutes (approx)

**1 packet of trifle sponges**
**700g of mixed fruit (raspberries, strawberries, blackberries)**
**300ml cream, whipped**
**Flaked Almonds**

**For the custard:**
**1 vanilla pod**
**pint of full fat milk**
**50g sugar**
**6 eggs yolks**

To make the Custard put the milk and vanilla pod in to a saucepan and slowly bring to the boil.

Beat the egg yolks and the sugar together. Slowly add the egg mixture to the milk, keep stirring until the custard thickens.

Line the bottom of the glasses with the sponges, add your berries (holding back a hand full for the top). When the custard has cooled pour it over the berries, then add the whipped cream.

Scatter the remaining berries on the top and serve!

DEDICATED TO: CUNNINGHAM'S SUPERVALU, RATOATH
NOMINATED LOCAL CHARITY: RATOATH ST VINCENT DE PAUL SOCIETY

# Joan Burke's BBQ Bananas

I've made this at our BBQ's for years! It's a firm favourite with family and friends and perfect on a hot summers evening!

Serves: 4
Preparation time: 5 minutes
Cooking time: 10-15 minutes

**4 bananas**
**½ tsp each ground nutmeg, ground ginger and ground cinnamon**
**Lemon juice (Approx ½ lemon)**
**8 small knobs of butter**
**Honey for drizzling**

Cut 4 rectangular pieces of tin foil and make each sheet into a gondola shape, big enough to hold the banana

Place the bananas in the gondolas

Brush the banana with lemon juice and sprinkle with the spices

Place a knob of butter at each end of the bananas and finally drizzle with honey to your taste

Close the tinfoil and place on a hot BBQ for 10 minutes (or until the banana is soft)

Serve with ice cream and enjoy!

Top Tips
Kids will love helping to prepare this fun dish, so make sure to get them involved!

HEALY'S SUPERVALU, DUNSHAUGHLIN
NOMINATED LOCAL CHARITY: ST VINCENT DE PAUL, DUNSHAUGHLIN

# Mabel Burns' After Eight Roulade

I find roulades a gift when entertaining. They look and taste spectacular!

Serves: 4 - 6
Preparation time: 30 minutes
Cooking time: 20 minutes

**Oil for greasing**
**Flour for dusting**
**5 eggs, separated**
175g / 6oz caster sugar
175g / 6oz plain chocolate chips
25g / 1oz After Eight mints
1 tbsp instant coffee granules
3 tbsp boiling water
Icing sugar for dredging
300mls / half pint double cream, whipped
5 After Eight mints cut into small squares

**For the decoration**
150mls / ¼ pint double cream, whipped
3 After Eight mints cut into triangles
Mint leaves

Pre-heat the oven to 375°F/ 190°C/ Gas 5

Line a 33cm x 23cm swiss roll tin with oiled and floured greaseproof paper sticking well up the sides

Whisk the yolks and sugar together until they leave a thin ribbon trail from the whisk

Melt the chocolate, coffee and After Eights in the water over a pan of simmering water. Fold the chocolate mixture into the whisked yolks and sugar

Whisk the whites until stiff and fold in. Spread the mixture evenly in the tin. Bake for 20 minutes until the top is dry to the touch and an inserted skewer comes out clean

Place the roulade in the tin on a cooling rack and cover with a just damp tea cloth to cool for 2 hours. Dredge a sheet of greaseproof paper with icing sugar. Flip the cake onto the greaseproof paper. Trim the edges. Peel away the lining paper

Spread with cream leaving a 4cm border along the short edge, dot with tiny squares of the mints and roll up removing paper as you go. Pipe the double whipped cream along the length of the roulade. Place the mint triangles in between the piped cream and decorate with mint leaves

MCCONVILLE'S SUPERVALU, PORTARLINGTON
NOMINATED LOCAL CHARITY: SPECIAL OLYMPICS IN
PORTARLINGTON

180

# David Donnelly's Layered Apple Crumble with Chantilly Cream and Caramel Sauce

My granny's speciality was apple crumble. I've now given it the layered treatment with Chantilly Cream. Irresistible!

Serves: 4
Preparation time: 25 minutes
Cooking time: 15-20 minutes

**Crumble:**
**2 medium cooking apples**
**150g self raising flour**
**100g caster sugar**
**2 level tsp cinnamon**
**30g pecan nuts, chopped**
**50g butter, and extra for greasing**

**Cream:**
**250ml whipped cream**
**2 tsp icing sugar**
**seeds from 2 vanilla pods**

**Caramel Sauce:**
**20g butter**
**4 tbsp caster sugar**
**3 tbsp pouring cream**
**2 eating apples**

Preheat the oven to 190°C (fan oven).

Grease 4 ramekins with butter.

Sieve flour and cinnamon into a large bowl. Rub in 50g butter until it looks like breadcrumbs.

Add half of the caster sugar and pecan nuts and mix well. Set aside.

Peel, core and chop cooking apples.

Add a layer of cooking apples to the ramekins and sprinkle with half the remaining caster sugar. Add a layer of crumble mix, then repeat each layer once, finishing with a crumble topping.

Bake in the oven for 15 minutes

Meanwhile, for the cream, mix the vanilla seeds (reserving the pods) with the whipped cream and icing sugar, and refrigerate until needed.

For the sauce, melt the butter in a pan, add the sugar and pouring cream, and allow to simmer down gently for 4-5 minutes to form a caramel.

Meanwhile, peel eating apples and scoop out balls using a melon scoop. Add the apple balls to the caramel and cook in the pan until the sauce is golden brown.

To serve, remove the crumbles from the ramekins and place in the centre of large plate. Pour the apple balls sauce around the crumble.

Put a dollop of the cream mix on each crumble and garnish with the reserved vanilla pods.

Tip
Leave apple pieces in water and apple juice so they don't brown

GUS O'GORMAN'S SUPERVALU, CARRICKMACROSS
NOMINATED LOCAL CHARITY: CARRICKMACROSS CANCER
FUND

# Hazel Whitaker Boozy Chocolate Trifle

Made with fresh raspberries from the garden, delicious!

Serves: 8
Preparation time: 20 minutes
Freezing time: 45 minutes
Cooking time: 10 minutes

**12 mini chocolate rolls**
**8 tbsp Baileys**
**11 oz white chocolate**
**1½ pints double cream**
**400g tub custard sauce**
**8 oz frozen or fresh raspberries**
**1 tbsp icing sugar**
**For decoration: 2 oz plain chocolate, 2 oz white**
**chocolate, 2 oz chopped marshmallows**

Divide each mini roll into 4 slices

Line 8 individual dishes with these slices. Drizzle with half of the Baileys

Break white chocolate into pieces and melt over a pot of boiling water. Stir until melted and then remove from the heat and allow to cool slightly

Whisk cream into soft peaks, then fold ⅓ of it into the melted white chocolate

Add custard and remaining Baileys and combine over the heat. Do not overcook or it will go lumpy

Divide the raspberries between the 8 dishes and sprinkle with icing sugar

Pour the custard mixture over it and put in the freezer for 45 minutes

Melt the decoration plain chocolate and spread over a plastic board. Allow to cool

Melt the decoration white chocolate and pour over the plain chocolate. Make curls from this using a vegetable peeler or grater

Remove dishes from the freezer, add the remaining whipped cream and decorate with chocolate curls

CAULFIELD'S SUPERVALU, MERCHANTS QUAY
NOMINATED LOCAL CHARITY: SHINE-IRISH PROGRESSIVE
ASSOCIATION FOR AUTISM

# Teresa Grant's Chocolate Mousse

This dessert goes down well with adults and children alike.
Serve with fruit salad, strawberries or ice cream

Serves: 8 - 10
Preparation time: 10 minutes
Chilling time: 4 hours

**275g mix plain and milk chocolate**
**175g castor sugar**
**6 eggs, separated**
**1 tbsp fresh cream**
**1 tbsp freshly squeezed orange juice**
**¼ tsp cocoa powder**
**¼ tsp sherry (optional)**

Melt chocolate in a bowl over a pan of simmering water

Beat egg yolks and 75g castor sugar until pale and creamy

Add the melted chocolate, cocoa powder, cream, orange juice and sherry

Continue whisking slowly

Wash whisk, then whisk egg whites with remaining sugar until stiff (in a seperate bowl)

Fold this into the chocolate mixture

Chill for 4 hours

Remember: Mousse contains raw egg so be carefull, particularly for pregnant women and young children

DALY'S SUPERVALU, TALLAGHT
NOMINATED LOCAL CHARITY: TALLAGHT CHILDREN'S HOSPITAL

# Tina Breen's Espresso Tiramisu

An old Italian friend introduced me to 'Tiramisu'. Flavoured with espresso and brandy it lives up to it's name – Italian for 'Pick me up'

Serves: 8 - 12
Preparation time: 30 minutes
Cooking time: 20 minutes

**Sponge:**
**4 oz flour**
**4 oz sugar**
**4 eggs**
**Pinch of espresso powder (instant)**

**Filling:**
**2 packets of cream cheese (8oz each)**
**12 oz icing sugar**
**12 oz heavy cream**
**3 tbsp brandy**
**1 tbsp espresso powder (instant)**

**Garnish:**
**Cocoa powder**

Preheat oven to 200°C

Dust 2 springform 9" sponge tins with flour

Beat eggs and sugar until light and fluffy

Fold in flour and espresso powder

Pour the mixture into tins and cook in the oven until brown and spongy to touch (15-20 minutes)

Meanwhile beat cream cheese and icing sugar together until creamy

Beat in the heavy cream, brandy and espresso powder until thick. Turn the cakes out of the tins

Cover the first cake layer with filling and top with the second cake layer

Cover the top and sides with remaining filling

Dust with cocoa powder and chill until ready to serve

GARVEY'S SUPERVALU, NEWCASTLEWEST
NOMINATED LOCAL CHARITY: THE AISLING GROUP

# Claire Mallon's Pavlova

For special occasions I am always asked to make my pavlova – it works every time

Serves: 8 - 10
Preparation time: 40 minutes
Cooking time: 1½ hours

**4 large egg whites**
**8oz castor sugar**
**Pinch of cream of tartar**
**1 tsp white wine vinegar**
**2 tsp cornflour**
**Pinch salt**
**2 drops vanilla extract**

**For the topping:**
**2 tbsp Cointreau**
**Punnet strawberries**
**100g white chocolate**
**125 ml whipped cream**

Preheat the oven to 300°F/ 150°C/ Gas 2

Whisk the egg whites until stiff. Add the sugar a tablespoon at a time whisking until the meringue is very stiff. Add the remaining ingredients and whisk in

Pile the meringue onto a baking sheet lined with parchment and spread into a 9 inch circle. Hollow out the centre slightly and bake in the oven for 1¼ hours
NB just before putting the meringue in turn the oven down to 120°C

When the cooking time is over, turn off the oven and leave the pavlova in the oven to cool.

*TIP – I usually make my pavlova the night before so it cools in the oven overnight*

Wash and prepare the strawberries and place in a bowl with the Cointreau or any other orange liquor and set aside for about 1 hour at room temperature.

Meanwhile chop the white chocolate into small chunks and whip the cream. Fold the strawberries and chocolate into the cream and pile into the centre of the pavlova

Cut into 8 – 10 slices and serve with the reserved Cointreau from the strawberries

*Tip: To use the egg yolks when making my pavlova I always make a custard based ice cream so there is no wastage.*

DOHERTY'S SUPERVALU, MAIN ST CARNDONAGH
NOMINATED LOCAL CHARITY: THE AISLING GROUP

# Rita Carolan's Bailey's Cheesecake

A family favourite – my aunt used to make this and shared the recipe with me

Serves: 6 - 8
Preparation time: 30 minutes
Chilling time: 3 hours

**8 oz chocolate digestive biscuits**
**3 oz butter**
**7 oz Philadelphia cheese**
**6 oz icing sugar**
**2 dsp Bailey's**
**medium carton of cream**

Melt butter and crush biscuits. Mix together well

Press into an 8 inch spring form tin and allow to cool

Beat cheese and sugar together

Beat cream until stiff, fold into cheese mixture with the Bailey's

Spread the mixture on top of the biscuit base

Leave in the fridge to set for approx 3 hours

Decorate with grated chocolate

Serve with strawberries or mixed berries

COMASKEY'S SUPERVALU, CLONES
NOMINATED LOCAL CHARITY: CLONES HOSPICE

# Phyllis Fennin's Lovely Light Sponge

I've won prizes with this never fails fresh cream sponge

Serves: 6 - 8
Preparation time: 10 - 12 minutes
Cooking time: 30 - 35 minutes

**4 eggs, separated**
**4 oz caster sugar**
**2 oz plain flour**
**2 oz corn flour**
**pinch of salt**
**level tsp baking powder**
**jam and cream for filling**

Whip the egg whites until they are stiff

Add in caster sugar and whip again until stiff

Add egg yolks, then whip again for about 5 minutes until stiff

Sieve flour, cornflour, salt and baking powder, and stir into egg mixture. Do not beat these in

Pour the mixture into 2 x 8" cake tins and place in a preheated oven 400° F/ 200° C/ Gas 6

Bake for about 30 minutes

Remove from the oven, allow to cool and turn out of cake tins. Sandwich the two halves together with your favourite filling, such as jam and cream, dust with icing sugar and cut into large wedges. Enjoy!

TIERNAN'S SUPERVALU, ATHY
NOMINATED LOCAL CHARITY: ST VINCENT DE PAUL

# Debbie Doyle's Berry Pie

My friend Michelle made this for my daughter's Communion – it was a winner!

Serves: 6 - 8
Preparation time: 20 minutes
Chilling time: 3-4 hours or overnight

**300g packet of ginger nut biscuits, crushed**
**75g butter, melted**
**120g caster sugar**
**whites of 2 large eggs**
**1 punnet of raspberries, rinsed plus extra for serving**
**285ml double cream, plus extra for serving**
**25cm spring form cake tin**

Freeze the cake tin (25cm spring form cake tin).

Mix the crushed biscuits with the melted butter and press into the base of the tin.

Return the tin to the freezer to set while you prepare the topping.

Combine the caster sugar, egg whites and raspberries in a bowl and beat with an electric mixer for about 10 minutes until pale and slightly stiff.

Whip the cream and stir it into the egg mixture.

Spoon the mixture onto the biscuit base and refrigerate until set, ideally overnight.

To serve, remove the pie from the tin by running a hot knife around the edge before opening the spring form.

Place on a plate, top with a few more raspberries and drizzle with a little cream.

SMITH'S SUPERVALU, NAVAN
NOMINATED LOCAL CHARITY: NAVAN MEALS ON WHEELS

# Rosaleen McHugh's Apricot Upside Down Cake

I first tasted apricots at the age of 11 when I babysat for my neighbour. I've loved them ever since!

Serves: 6
Preparation time: 20 minutes
Cooking time: 50 minutes

**6 oz (190g) butter**
**6 oz (190g) caster sugar**
**6 oz (190g) self raising flour**
**1½ x 411g tins of apricot halves, drained**
**3 medium eggs**
**a few drops vanilla essence**
**3 tbsp caster sugar to decorate**

Preheat oven to 350°F/ 180°C/ Gas 4

Grease an 8"/20cm round loose based cake tin, then line the base with greaseproof paper.

Mix a knob of butter with 2 tablespoons of caster sugar, spread over the greaseproof base, then line with apricot halves.

Place the remaining butter and sugar in a large mixing bowl, sift in the flour, add the eggs and vanilla essence.

Beat all the ingredients until smooth. Spoon the cake mix over the apricot halves.

Bake for 50 minutes until golden brown. Allow the cake to stand for 10 minutes, then turn out of the tin so that the fruit is on top.

Sprinkle the caster sugar over the apricots, then place under the grill for 2-3 minutes until the sugar melts.

Remove from under the grill, allow to cool and serve.

KAVANAGH''S SUPERVALU, KILTIMAGH
NOMINATED LOCAL CHARITY: CASTLEBAR MRI SCANNER FUND

# Catriona Connolly's Whiskey & Baileys Sponge Cake

Everyone who eats this cake just loves it! They all think it must be difficult to make as it's so delicious – but my secret is out as it's actually very easy!

Serves: 10
Preparation time: 25 minutes + cooling time
Cooking time: 10-15 minutes

**8 eggs**
**8 oz caster sugar**
**8 oz self raising flour**
**1 tsp vanilla essence**
**411g tin of peach slices**
**3 tbsp raspberry jam**
**8-10 tbsp of whiskey**
**225ml double cream**
**1 tsp sugar**
**4 tbsp Baileys**
**50g chocolate**

To make sponge: Beat eggs and sugar until very light and fluffy. Slowly fold in flour and add vanilla essence.

Divide mixture between two greased 8" cake tins and bake in a pre-heated oven at 180°C for approximately 12-15 minutes. Remove from oven and allow to cool.

Meanwhile, drain the peaches and mix with approx five tablespoons of the whiskey, leaving to one side to marinade a little

Mix the jam with the remaining whiskey and spread this mixture on one side of each of the cooled sponges.

Spoon the marinated peaches onto the jam covered sponges.

Beat the cream with a little sugar until very stiff. Add the Baileys and beat again (should be the colour of toffee). Spread this on top of the peaches on each sponge.

Sandwich the two sponges together so that there is jam, peaches and cream in the middle and on the top of the cake, grate chocolate on top.

Best refrigerated for 2 to 3 hours before serving. Slice into chunky wedges and enjoy!

MCCONNON'S SUPERVALU, CASTLEBLANEY
NOMINATED LOCAL CHARITY: CASTLEBLANEY CANCER UNIT

# Mary Jenkins' Strawberry Shortcake Gateau

This is a nice summer gateau when strawberries are in season and a must for a special occasion.

Serves: 8-10
Preparation time: 30 minutes + 2½ hours chillling time
Cooking time: 15 minutes

**For the shortcake:**
**8 oz caster sugar**
**9 oz butter**
**3 beaten eggs**
**1 lb 2 oz flour (sifted)**

**For the mousse:**
**12 oz strawberries**
**3 oz caster sugar**
**3 tbsp orange juice**
**1 sachet powdered gelatine**
**½ pint double cream**
**1 egg white**
**icing for dusting**

For the shortcake, put the sugar and butter in a bowl and beat until fluffy. Add the eggs. Stir in the flour to make a dough. Knead lightly, wrap in cling film and chill for 15 minutes.

Preheat oven to 180°C/ 350°F/ gas 4.

Divide the dough into 3 and roll out each piece on a sheet of parchment paper, into a 9" round. Transfer still on baking parchment to baking trays. Prick all over. Chill for at least 30 minutes.

Bake the chilled shortcake rounds for 15-20 minutes until crisp and golden. Remove from the oven, and while still hot trim the shortcake with a sharp knife using the base of a loose bottomed 8" tin as a guide. Carefully remove from baking parchment using a palette knife and leave to cool on a wire rack.

Meanwhile, reserve 2 oz of strawberries and purée the rest.

In a bowl, dissolve the sugar in 4 tablespoons of boiling water. Add the orange juice and sprinkle the gelatine over the top. Stir until dissolved. Stir into the strawberry purée and reserve. Whisk the egg white until holding soft peaks. In a separate bowl, whisk the cream to soft peaks, and fold both this and the egg white into the strawberry mixture to make a mousse. Layer the shortcake discs and the mousse in the 8" cake tin used earlier, starting and finishing with shortcake. Chill for at least two hours until firm then remove from tin. Dust with icing sugar. Halve the reserved strawberries and decorate the top with them.

JONES' SUPERVALU, CLONMEL
NOMINATED LOCAL CHARITY: CUAN SAOR

# Máirín Uí Thuairisg's Chocolate Cake

This recipe is easy, fast and tastes good. It's great if you're having company or if you keep Irish students which a lot of people do here in the Gaeltacht. I got this recipe from a dear friend from Spain and gave it my own twist

Serves: 12
Preparation time: 20 minutes
Cooking time: 45 minutes

**Cake:**
**3 cups of self raising flour**
**2 cups of caster sugar**
**½ cup of cocoa powder**
**2 cups of water**
**¾ cup Flora oil, and extra for greasing**
**2 tbsp vinegar**
**2 tbsp vanilla essence**

**Icing:**
**1 cup of caster sugar**
**¼ cup of cocoa powder**
**¼ cup of butter**
**¼ cup of milk**

Preheat the oven to 180°C. Sift the flour, sugar and cocoa powder together.

Slowly add the wet ingredients (water, Flora oil, vinegar, vanilla) and mix well.

Pour the mixture into a greased 10" x 12" pan and pop into the preheated oven. Cook for approximately 45 minutes.

Remove from the oven and allow to cool on a wire rack.

Meanwhile, to make the icing, add the sugar, cocoa powder, butter and milk to a saucepan and melt over a moderate heat.

Allow to boil for one minute.

Remove the pan from the heat and pour this icing over the cooled cake.

Cut the cake into squares and serve with cream or ice cream.

KERRIGAN'S SUPERVALU, INDREABHÁN
NOMINATED LOCAL CHARITY: TO RUSSIA WITH LOVE

# Sinéad Keogh's Cacá Mílís

A luxurious chocolate cake – no cake quite like it as it's my own original recipe!

Serves: 6
Preparation time: 20 minutes
Cooking time: 25 minutes

**200g brown sugar**
**200g margarine**
**175g self raising flour**
**50g Cadbury cocoa powder**
**2 eggs**
**¼ pint sour cream**

**For the filling and icing:**
**400g icing sugar**
**100g butter**
**100g cocoa powder**
**4 tsp milk**

Cream together the margarine and sugar until light and fluffy

Beat the 2 eggs and sour cream, add to the creamed mixture and mix

Sieve the flour and cocoa together, add to the mixture and beat until fluffy

Divide mixture equally between two 8 inch round cake tins

Bake in a preheated oven at 190°C/375°F/gas 5 for 25 minutes. Remove and cool on a wire rack

For the filling and icing: Melt butter in a large saucepan, add milk and stir

Sieve cocoa and icing sugar together. Add to saucepan and beat until velvety

Add more milk if lighter fudge taste is required

Use this icing to sandwich the cake together. Cover the sides and top with the remaining icing

Leave to set

Serve in slices with whipped cream or ice cream

PETTITT'S SUPERVALU, ARKLOW
NOMINATED LOCAL CHARITY: IRISH WHEELCHAIR
ASSOCIATION ARKLOW

# Gillian Coyle's Lemon Curd Roulade

This is a lemon meringue pie without the pastry – suitable for coeliacs

Makes 1 roulade
Preparation time: 30 minutes
Cooking time: 25 minutes

**Meringue Base:**
**2 tbsp cornflour**
**250g white caster sugar**
**4 egg whites (at room temperature)**
**1 tsp vanilla essence**

**Lemon Curd:**
**3 lemons**
**100g unsalted butter**
**73g caster sugar**
**4 egg yolks**
**3 tbsp cornflour mixed into a mug of water**

**½ pint cream to decorate**

To make the base:
Add the cornflour to the sugar. Whisk the egg whites in a glass bowl. When nearly stiff add vanilla and gradually add the sugar and cornflour. Whisk until stiff peaks form.

Spread the mixture out onto a baking tray lined with parchment.

Bake in a preheated oven at 170°C for 25 minutes – it should be crisp on top with a soft middle. Leave to cool in tin.

For the lemon curd; zest the lemon skins onto a plate (keep aside 1 tsp for garnishing).

Cut the lemons in half and juice (strain for pips).

In a heavy based saucepan put the butter, sugar, lemon juice, lemon zest, egg yolks and water with the cornflour.

Over a very low heat use a whisk to stir the mixture until all ingredients have melted.

Continue whisking until it beings to thicken, when thick remove from the heat. You should have a thick smooth sauce. Allow to cool.

To make the Roulade:
On a kitchen counter or tray, invert the meringue base onto a clean tea towel, one side of long edge to the edge of the tea towel – the smooth side will now be on top, and crispy side underneath.

Mix half the whipped cream with the lemon curd and spread over the base.

From the side with the most tea towel showing, roll the base over on itself Swiss roll style.

Spread the remaining cream on top and garnish with lemon zest and sieved icing sugar.

# Gretta Meehan's Syrup Pudding

My granny made this pudding every Saturday night. It tastes just as good now as it did then!

Serves: 8 approximately
Preparation time: 15 minutes
Cooking time: 1 hour

**1 tsp bread soda**
**1 tsp caster sugar**
**1 cup breadcrumbs**
**1 cup flour**
**¼ lb currants**
**1 tsp ground cinnamon**
**½ lb margarine**
**1 cup buttermilk**
**1 tsp golden syrup**

**Sauce:**
**1 dsp cornflour**
**1 tbsp caster sugar**
**1 cup milk**
**a little nutmeg**

In a bowl combine bread soda, sugar, breadcrumbs, flour, currants and cinnamon with the margarine.

Mix together the buttermilk and syrup and then add to the dry ingredients, mixing throughly.

Pour the mixture into a 1 pint pudding bowl and cover with greaseproof paper.

Steam the pudding for 1 hour – this can be done in a steamer or in a pot of water (make sure the water only comes half way up the bowl), with the bowl set on an upturned heatproof saucer.

Meanwhile, to make the sauce combine all of the sauce ingredients in a saucepan and bring to the boil over a moderate heat, stirring continuously.

Serve a slice of the pudding in a bowl generously topped with the sauce.

DONOHOE'S SUPERVALU, BALLINAMORE
NOMINATED LOCAL CHARITY: LOCAL TIDY TOWNS
COMMITTEE

# Barbara Flood's Bread and Butter Pudding

Our mother used to make this for us years ago. It was a great way to use up 'not so fresh' bread. I have added a few extras to the recipe to give it a touch of luxury

Serves: 4
Preparation time: 30 minutes
Cooking time: 40-45 minutes

**6 slices of bread (white or brown)**
**½ pint/300 ml of milk**
**2 eggs**
**50g butter**
**75g sugar**
**175g sultanas**
**½ tbsp port (optional)**
**250g mixed berries**
**Fresh cream (optional)**

Preheat the oven to 180°C. Soak the sultanas in the port. Meanwhile lightly oil a 2-2½ pint dish

Remove crusts from bread, spread with butter and cut into small pieces. Place a layer of bread on the bottom of the dish. Next, place a layer of the sultanas on top

Whisk together the eggs, milk and sugar and pour over the sultanas in the dish. Leave to soak for 20 minutes

Bake in the oven for approx 40 minutes

When cooked scatter with mixed berries and serve with whipped cream

NALLY'S SUPERVALU, TRIM
NOMINATED LOCAL CHARITY: TRIM ARCH CLUB

# Geraldine Daly's Economical Lemon Cheesecake

My mother used this recipe when cheesecakes first became popular but were very expensive to make. She first used this recipe about 15 years ago and it's still delicious today

Serves: 7
Preparation time: 20 minutes (plus chilling time)

**4-6 ozs digestive biscuits**
**3 ozs butter**

**Filling:**
**6 ozs Philadelphia cream cheese(plain)**
**2 ozs castor sugar.**
**1 lemon**
**1 pack of lemon jelly**
**½ pint boiling water**
**¼ pint cream**

**To decorate:**
**Whipped cream & grapes**

Crumble biscuits by placing them in a plastic bag and crushing with a rolling pin until completely broken. Melt butter, add to crumbled biscuits, and press into 8" false bottom tin. Leave in fridge. Add jelly to the boiling water and leave to cool. Mix cheese, castor sugar, rind and juice of lemon together. This mixture must be mixed very well, try and get out all lumps. Mixing takes about 10 minutes (If you leave the cheese out of the fridge for a few hours it is easier to mix). When mixture is ready add the cooled jelly, stir and leave in fridge until nearly set. Remove from fridge. Lightly beat 1/4 pint of cream and fold into mixture. Pour mixture onto biscuit base and leave in fridge to set. When set decorate with green/black grapes and whipped cream. If you use a false bottom tin, you can push cheesecake up which makes it easier to remove.

BUCKLEY'S SUPERVALU, BIRR
NOMINATED LOCAL CHARITY: ST VINCENT DE PAUL

# Clodagh McKenna's Spiced Poached Pears

Serves: 6 approximately
Preparation time: 10 minutes
Cooking time: 15 - 20 minutes

**500ml red wine**
**500g caster sugar**
**2kg pears**
**2 cinnamon sticks**
**4 star anise**

Put the red wine and sugar in a large pan and cook over a low heat until the sugar has dissolved. Peel, quarter, and core the pears. Add to the wine with the cinnamon sticks and star anise. Leave over a medium heat for a further 10 minutes or until tender. Transfer to sterilised kilner or jam jars.

TIP: Delicious served with whipped cream or ice cream or sliced over a flan.

DEDICATED TO: CONDRON'S SUPERVALU, TALLAGHT
NOMINATED LOCAL CHARITY: LOCAL MEALS ON WHEELS

# Chef Phelim Byrne's Roast Fruits and Mixed Berry Compote

Serves: 4
Preparation time: 10 - 15 minutes
Cooking time: 20 - 25 minutes

**Berry Compote:**
**1 cup mixed berries fresh or frozen**
**1 tbsp caster sugar**
**a dash of brandy**

**Roast Fruits:**
**2 pears**
**2 apples**
**2 peaches**
**3 tbsp honey**
**2 tbsp brown sugar**

**To serve:**
**250g mascarpone**
**2-3 drops vanilla essence or seeds of ½ vanilla pod**

Simply heat a frying pan, add the fruits and sugar with the dash of alcohol. Over a high heat quickly toss the fruits around the pan for about 30 seconds until the sugar is almost all dissolved. Pour into a serving dish and leave to cool.

I like pear, apple and fresh peaches cut into quarters for this one. Place on a tray with some honey and brown sugar and place in the oven for about 20 minutes until just caramelised at 200°C. Cool slightly. On a large plate place 2 pieces each of the fruit in the centre, spoon some of the berry compote round the plate. Meanwhile mix the mascarpone with the vanilla essence or seeds and place a spoon of this on top of the fruits. Drizzle around the plate also.

DEDICATED TO: SMYTH'S SUPERVALU, BALLYMAHON
NOMINATED LOCAL CHARITY: SOCIETY FOR PREVENTION OF CRUELTY TO ANIMALS

# Eleanor Whyte's Fruit Pudding

Something I created from tins of fruit I had in the press. It's a little different as it has no extravagant ingredients!

Serves: 6
Preparation time: 15 minutes
Cooking time: 20 minutes

**1 tin of pears**
**1 tin of peaches**
**juice of 1 orange**
**1 cup of fruit juice (from the tins)**
**½ tsp cinnamon**
**1 tbsp honey**
**4 oz margarine**
**4 oz Demerara sugar**
**2 eggs**
**½ lb self raising flour**

Put the fruit, orange juice and tin juice in the base of an ovenproof dish.

Sprinkle the cinnamon and spoon the honey over the fruit.

In a separate bowl, cream the sugar and margarine together.

Beat the eggs, one at a time and then beat them into the creamed mixture.

Sieve the flour and fold into the mix.

Spread this mixture over the fruit and bake in a preheated oven at 200°C for approximately 20 minutes or until golden brown.

# Your local store and charity at a glance

## Carlow

Hickson's **SuperValu** Bridge Street, Tullow.
t: 059 9151132 Nominated Charity: Carlow/Kilkenny
Home Care Team

Byrne's **SuperValu** Main Street, Hacketstown.
t: 059 6471555 Nominated Charity: St Johns Daycare
Centre

Arthur's **SuperValu** 83 Tullow Street, Carlow.
t: 059 9131263 Nominated Charity: Holy Angels
Carlow

Connolly's **SuperValu** Pump Street, Bagenalstown,
Co Carlow. t: 059-9723000 Nominated Charity:
Carlow/Kilkenny Home Care Team

## Cavan

Foy's **SuperValu** 52 - 54 Market Street, Cootehill.
t: 049 5552122 Nominated Charity: Holy Family
School

Tarpey's **SuperValu** Dublin Road, Cavan Town.
t: 049 4375270 Nominated Charity: Cavan Parish
Drugs Awareness

Donohoe's **SuperValu** Realta Shopping Centre,
Ballyconnell t: 049 9526155 Nominated Charity:
Local Tidy Towns Committee

Harris' **SuperValu** Main Street, Baileborough.
t: 042 9665348 Nominated Charity: Baileborough
Cancer Fund

Carolan's **SuperValu** Kingscourt. t: 042 9667835
Nominated Charity: Cavan Hospice

## Clare

Queally's **SuperValu** Convent Hill, Killaloe
t: 061 620230 Nominated Charity: Killaloe/Ballina
Search and Rescue

Queally's **SuperValu** Francis Street, Kilrush.
t: 065 9051885 Nominated Charity: West Clare
Cancer Group

Fitzpatrick's **SuperValu** Parliament Street, Ennistymon.
t: 065 7071600 Nominated Charity: Friends of
Ennistymon Hospital

Lyons/Dunlon's **SuperValu** Main Street, Tulla.
t: 065 6835255 Nominated Charity: Clare
Cancer Society

Lannon/Lehane **SuperValu** Newmarket-on-Fergus.
t: 061 368036 Nominated Charity: Down
Syndrome Ireland

## Cork

Caulfield's **SuperValu** Merchant's Quay,
Cork City. t: 021 4279050 Nominated Charity:
SHINE - Irish Progressive Association for Autism

Brooke's **SuperValu** 143 North Main Street, Youghal.
t: 024 92279 Nominated Charity: Youghal Community
Hospital

Dano's **SuperValu** Bellevue Stores, Mallow.
t: 022 21662  Nominated Charity: Cope, Mallow

O'Keeffe's **SuperValu** Boherbue, Mallow.
t: 029 76105 Nominated Charity: Cope Kanturk and
St. Josephs Charleville

Riordan's **SuperValu** Courthouse Road, Fermoy.
t: 025 31275 Nominated Charity: Cope
Foundation, Fermoy

Ryan's **SuperValu** Crestfield Centre, Glanmire.
t: 021 4822500 Nominated Charity: Tir na N'Óg
Respite Services

Scally's **SuperValu** Fax Bridge, Cork Road, Clonakilty.
t: 023 33088 Nominated Charity: Cope Foundation

Ryan's **SuperValu** Grange Road, Frankfield.
t: 021 4890330 Nominated Charity: Tir na N'Óg
Respite Services

Singleton's **SuperValu** Hollyhill Shopping Centre,
Hollyhill. t: 021 4392555 Nominated Charity:
St. Marys on the Hill

Smith's **SuperValu** Long Quay, Kinsale.
t: 021 4772843 Nominated Charity: Kinsale Hospital

Down's **SuperValu** Main Street, Ballincollig.
t: 021 4870154 Nominated Charity: Brothers
of Charity

Collins' **SuperValu** Main Street, Carrigaline.
t: 021 4852244 Nominated Charity: Marymount
Hospice

Dick's **SuperValu** Main Street, Charleville.
t: 063 81277 Nominated Charity: St. Joseph's
Workshop

Healy's **SuperValu** Main Street, Dunmanway.
t: 023 45778 Nominated Charity: Dunmanway
Hospital

O'Leary's **SuperValu** Main Street, Macroom.
t: 026 41101 Nominated Charity: Macroom Hospital

Herlihy's **SuperValu** Main Street, Mallow.
t: 022 21159 Nominated Charity: Aisling Group

Field's **SuperValu** Main Street, Skibbereen.
t: 028 21400 Nominated Charity: Cope Foundation,
Skibbereen

Reidy's **SuperValu** New Square, Mitchelstown.
t: 025 86812 Nominated Charity:
Tearmonn Ui Chaoimh Day Care Centre

Bigg's **SuperValu** New Street, Bantry. t: 027 50001
Nominated Charity: Bantry Care for the Aged

**SuperValu** Newmarket Co-op. t: 029 60282
Nominated Charity: St Joseph's Foundation, Charleville

Caulfield's **SuperValu** Riverview Shopping Centre,
McSweeney Quay, Bandon. t: 023 29944
Nominated Charity: Hyperbaric Chamber Fund

Scally's **SuperValu** Skehard Road, Blackrock, Cork.
t: 021 4358819 Nominated Charity: Chernobyl
Greater Call

Twohig's **SuperValu** Strand Street, Kanturk.
t: 029 50069 Nominated Charity: Kanturk Hospital

Murphy's **SuperValu** The Bridge, Castletownbere.
t: 027 70020 Nominated Charity:Castletownbere RNLI
Lifeboat

Ryan's **SuperValu** The Lough Shopping Centre,
Togher. t: 021 4313268 Nominated Charity:
Tir na N'Óg Respite Services

Collins' **SuperValu** The Square, Blarney.
t: 021 4385571 Nominated Charity: Marymount
Hospice

O'Keeffe's **SuperValu** The Square, Millstreet.
t: 029 70193 Nominated Charity: The Day Care
Centre, Millstreet

Garvey's **SuperValu** Tiknock, Cobh. t: 021 4908340
Nominated Charity: Cobh Community Centre

Hurley's **SuperValu** Towns Park, Mill Road, Midleton.
t: 021 4631570 Nominated Charity: Midleton Hospital

Quish's **SuperValu** West End, Ballincollig.
t: 021 4870719 Nominated Charity: Guide Dogs
Association

## Donegal

Kavanagh's **SuperValu** Cockhill Road, Buncrana.
t: 074 9361719 Nominated Charity: Cash na Cor
Resource Centre

Kavanagh's **SuperValu** Donegal Shopping Centre,
Donegal Town. t: 074 9722977 Nominated Charity:
Donegal Hospice, Donegal Town

Kavanagh's **SuperValu** Dungloe. t: 074 9521006
Nominated Charity: The Dungloe Hydropool
Building Fund

**SuperValu** Link Road, Letterkenny.
t: 074 9102270 Nominated Charity: Donegal Hospice

Doherty's **SuperValu** Main Street, Carndonagh.
t: 074 9329318 Nominated Charity: Aisling Group

## Dublin

Treacy's **SuperValu** 13 Braemor Road, Churchtown,
Dublin 14. t: 01 2984917 Nominated Charity:
Aisling Group

Kane & McCartney's **SuperValu** 167 Howth Road,
Killester, Dublin 3. t: 01 8332968 Nominated Charity:
Central Remedial Clinic Clontarf

Kiernan's **SuperValu** 27 The Rise, Mount Merrion,
Dublin 4. t: 01 2881014 Nominated Charity: Mount
Merrion Community Centre

Byrne's **SuperValu** Aston Quay, Dublin 2.
t: 01-6795422 Nominated Charity: Local Meals
on Wheels

Daly's **SuperValu** Aylesbury Shopping Centre,
Tallaght, Dublin 24. t: 01 4510038
Nominated Charity: Tallaght Children's Hospital

**SuperValu** Balally Shopping Centre, Sandyford,
Dublin 16. t: 01 2958330
Nominated Charity: Crumlin Children's Hospital

Moriarty's **SuperValu** Church Street, Skerries, Dublin.
t: 01 8493113 Nominated Charity: Local Meals
on Wheels

Murphy's **SuperValu** College View, Silogur Road,
Ballymun, Dublin 11. t: 01 8421681
Nominated Charity: St Francis Hospital, Raheny

Kane's **SuperValu** Donabate, Co Dublin.
t: 01 8436350 Nominated Charity: Irish
Cancer Society

Moriarty's **SuperValu** Drogheda Street, Balbriggan.
t: 01 8413874 Nominated Charity: Local Meals
on Wheels

Regan's **SuperValu** Firhouse Shopping Centre,
Tallaght, Dublin 24. t: 01 4522822
Nominated Charity: Harolds Cross Hospice

Dooley's **SuperValu** Fortunestown Shopping Centre,
Springfield, Tallaght, Dublin 24. t: 01 4599247
Nominated Charity: Local St. Vincent De Paul

McDonnell's **SuperValu** Lorcan Avenue, Santry,
Dublin 9. t: 01 8420020
Nominated Charity: St. Michaels House

Caulfield's **SuperValu** Main Street, Malahide.
t: 01 8450233 Nominated Charity: Casa Caring and
Sharing Association, Malahide

Horkan's **SuperValu** Orwell Shopping Centre,
Wellington Lane, Templeogue. t: 01 4567842
Nominated Charity: St. Michael's House

Moriarty's **SuperValu** Palmerstown Shopping Centre,
Kennelsfort Road, Dublin 20. t: 01 6260736
Nominated Charity: Local Meals on Wheels

Kane & McCartney's **SuperValu** Raheny Shopping
Centre, Raheny, Dublin 5. t: 01 8310013 Nominated
Charity: St Francis Hospice, Raheny

Coughlan's **SuperValu** Shankill Shopping Centre,
Shankill. t: 01 2826922 Nominated Charity: Local
St. Vincent De Paul

Casey's **SuperValu** Station Rd, Lusk. t: 01 8437673
Nominated Charity: Our Lady's Hospital, Crumlin

Kane's **SuperValu** Talbot Street, Dublin 1.
t: 01 8560927 Nominated Charity: Irish Cancer Society

Hanley's **SuperValu** Unit 1, Chaplins Court, Rowlagh
Village Centre, Neilstown Rd, Clondalkin.
t: 01 6200042 Nominated Charity: Local St. Vincent
De Paul

Twomey's **SuperValu**, Clonkeen Road, Deansgrange.
t: 01 2895149 Nominated Charity: Bernardo's

Condron's **SuperValu** Belgard Square West, Tallaght.
t: 01 4622111 Nominated Charity: Local Meals
on Wheels

O'Ciobhain's **SuperValu** Boroimhe Shopping Centre,
Forest Road, Swords. t: 01 8405560
Nominated Charity: Down Syndrome Ireland

## Galway

Nestor's **SuperValu** Ballybane Shopping Centre,
Ballybane. t: 091 751173 Nominated Charity:
Galway Hospice

O'Toole's **SuperValu** Bishop Street, Tuam.
t: 093 24800 Nominated Charity: Tuam Cancer Centre

Dunne's **SuperValu** Brackernagh, Ballinasloe.
t: 090 9644404 Nominated Charity: Aisling Group

Minihane's **SuperValu** Church Street, Gort.
t: 091 632784 Nominated Charity: South Galway
Social Services

O'Meara's **SuperValu** Clonfert Road, Portumna.
t: 090 9741143 Nominated Charity:
St Dympna School

Kerrigan's **SuperValu** Coill Rua, Indreabhán.
t: 091 593020 Nominated Charity: To Russia
with Love

Nestor's **SuperValu** Fr Griffin Road, Co Galway.
t: 091 588695 Nominated Charity: Galway Hospice

Clarke's **SuperValu** Freeport, Barna. t: 091 596507
Nominated Charity: Special Olympics

Heneghan's **SuperValu** Kilkerrin Road, Glenamaddy.
t: 094 9659645 Nominated Charity: Grá in Loughrea
(parent group for children with autism)

Kyne's **SuperValu** Moycullen. t: 091 555107
Nominated Charity: Voices for Galway

Flynn's **SuperValu** Lackagh, Turloughmore.
t: 091 797753 Nominated Charity: St. Vincent de Paul

Kavanagh's **SuperValu** Market Street, Clifden.
t: 095 21182 Nominated Charity: Clifden
District Hospital

Nestor's **SuperValu** Orantown Centre, Oranmore.
t: 091 792044 Nominated Charity: Galway Hospice

McInerney's **SuperValu** The Green, Loughrea.
t: 091 841006 Nominated Charity: Cancer Care West

## Kerry

Garvey's **SuperValu** Church Street, Castleisland.
t: 066 7142232 Nominated Charity: CastleIsland
Branch of the Kerry Hospice

Garvey's **SuperValu** Convent Street, Listowel.
t: 068 21385 Nominated Charity: Listowel Hospice

Garvey's **SuperValu** Holy Ground, Dingle.
t: 066 9151397 Nominated Charity: Aisling Group

Keane's **SuperValu** Iveragh Road, Killorglin.
t: 066 9762166 Nominated Charity: Aisling Group

Cahills' **SuperValu** Main Street, Ballybunion.
t: 068 27244 Nominated Charity: Local Tidy
Towns Committee

Murphy's **SuperValu** Main Street, Kenmare.
t: 064 41307 Nominated Charity: Kenmare Hospital

Daly's **SuperValu** Park Road, Killarney.
t: 064 31400 Nominated Charity: MS Society Killarney

Garvey's **SuperValu** Rock Street, Tralee.
t: 066 7122475 Nominated Charity: Tralee MS Society

Walsh's **SuperValu** Valentia Road, Cahirciveen.
t: 066 9472380 Nominated Charity: Cahirciveen Hospice

## Kildare

Condron's **SuperValu** Abbeylands Shopping Centre, Clane. t: 045 893200 Nominated Charity: Local Meals on Wheels

Tiernan's **SuperValu** Duke Street, Athy. t: 059 8638578 Nominated Charity: St. Vincent de Paul

Pettitt's **SuperValu** Edmund Rice Square, Athy. t: 059 8638645 Nominated Charity: Alzheimer's Unit, St. Vincent's Hospital, Athy

Kenna's **SuperValu** Glen Royal Shopping Centre, Maynooth. t: 01 6290932 Nominated Charity: Crumlin Hospital

Murphy's **SuperValu** River Forest Shopping Centre, Captain's Hill, Leixlip. t: 01 6245118 Nominated Charity: Irish Heart Foundation

McConville's **SuperValu** Shopping Centre, Monasterevin. t: 045 525487 Nominated Charity: Monasterevin Special Olympics Committee

Reilly's **SuperValu** Sallins, Co. Kildare. t: 045 853711 Nominated Charity: Aisling Group

## Kilkenny

Dick's **SuperValu** Castle Street, Ballyragget. t: 056 8833122 Nominated Charity: New Horizons, School for Autism, Goresbridge

Caulfield's **SuperValu** Loughboy Shopping Centre, Loughboy. t: 056 7765404 Nominated Charity: Kilkenny SOS

Crehan & McCabe's **SuperValu** Main Street, Callan. t: 056 7725603 Nominated Charity: Special Olympics

Doran's **SuperValu** Main Street, Graiguenamagh. t: 059 9724452 Nominated Charity: Gahan House Home

Kavanagh's **SuperValu** Dublin Rd, Thomastown. t: 056 7724175 Nominated Charity: Aisling Group

## Laois

Cahalan's **SuperValu** Main Street, Abbeyleix. t: 057 8731606 Nominated Charity: Abbeyleix District Hospital

McConville's **SuperValu** Main Street, Portarlington. t: 057 8623178 Nominated Charity: Special Olympics in Portarlington

Delaney's **SuperValu** The Ossory, Rathdowney. t: 0505 46334 Nominated Charity: Aisling Group

## Leitrim

Donohoe's **SuperValu** Main Street, Ballinamore. t: 071 9644609 Nominated Charity: Local Tidy Town

Glancy's **SuperValu** Sligo Road, Carrick-on-Shannon. t: 071 9621010 Nominated Charity: Conquer Cancer

## Limerick

Twohig's **SuperValu** Abbeyfeale. t: 068 31407 Nominated Charity: Aisling Group

Dooley's **SuperValu** Bishops Street, Newcastlewest. t: 069 62158 Nominated Charity: St. Vincent de Paul NCW

Garvey's **SuperValu** Grove Island, Corbally. t: 061 350200 Nominated Charity: Milford Hospice

Ryan's **SuperValu** Sarsfield Street, Kilmallock. t: 063 98336 Nominated Charity: Tir na N'Óg Respite Services

Garvey's **SuperValu** The Square, Newcastlewest. t: 069 61312 Nominated Charity: Aisling Group

Lehane's **SuperValu** Watchhouse Cross, Parteen Road, Limerick. t: 061 455204 Nominated Charity: Down Syndrome Ireland

## Longford

Dunphy's **SuperValu** Barrack Street, Granard. t: 043 86375 Nominated Charity: St. Christophers, Longford

Duffy's **SuperValu** Edgeworthstown. t: 043 71162 Nominated Charity: Local Tidy Towns

Smyth's **SuperValu** Main Street, Ballymahon. t: 090 6432376. Nominated Charity: Society for Prevention of Cruelty to Animals

Davis' **SuperValu** Hazelwood Shopping Centre, Longford. t: 043 46339 Nominated Charity: Longford Hospice

## Louth

Lanney's **SuperValu** Ardee. t: 041 6853322 Nominated Charity: Ardee Hospice

Kane & McCartney's **SuperValu** Stockwell Avenue, Drogheda. t: 041 9842057 Nominated Charity: St. Vincent de Paul, Drogheda

## Mayo

Sweeney's **SuperValu** Achill Sound. t: 098 45211 Nominated Charity: Achill Branch of Croí

Moloney's **SuperValu** Bunree, Ballina. t: 096 24644 Nominated Charity: Aisling Group

Kavanagh's **SuperValu** Claremorris. t: 094 9362242 Nominated Charity: St. Rita's

Kavanagh's **SuperValu** Kiltimagh. t: 094 9381654 Nominated Charity: Castlebar MRI Scanner Fund

Kavanagh's **SuperValu** New Antrim Street, Castlebar. t: 094 9024808 Nominated Charity: Bright Eyes

Cummins' **SuperValu** New Street, Ballinrobe. t: 094 9541614 Nominated Charity: Western Care

Ryan's **SuperValu** Newpark, Ballyhaunis. t: 094 9630359 Nominated Charity: Mayo Roscommon Hospice

Kavanagh's **SuperValu** Shop Street, Westport. t: 098 27000 Nominated Charity: St. Vincent de Paul

## Meath

O'Brien's **SuperValu** 1/1A Kells Shopping Centre, Kells. t: 046 9240983 Nominated Charity: St. Vincent de Paul

Bird's **SuperValu** Beachmount Shopping Centre, Navan. t: 046 9023800 Nominated Charity: Local Meals on Wheels

Cunningham's **SuperValu** Fairyhouse Road, Ratoath. t: 01 8257800 Nominated Charity: Ratoath St Vincent de Paul Society

Nally's **SuperValu** Haggard Street, Trim. t: 046 9431505 Nominated Charity: Trim Arch Club

Smith's **SuperValu** Johnstown Centre, Johnstown, Navan. t: 046 9091086 Nominated Charity: Navan Meals on Wheels

Healy's **SuperValu** The Gables, Dunshaughlin Shopping Centre, Dunshaughlin. t: 01 8259711 Nominated Charity: St. Vincent de Paul, Dunsaughlin

Cadden's **SuperValu** The Square, Oldcastle. t: 049 8541131 Nominated Charity: Aisling Group

Molloy's **SuperValu** Town Centre, Ashbourne. t: 01 8352186 Nominated Charity: Local Meals on Wheels

## Monaghan

Comaskey's **SuperValu** Fermanagh Street, Clones.
t: 047 51089 Nominated Charity: Clones Hospice

McConnon's **SuperValu** Main Street, Castleblayney
t: 042 9746005 Nominated Charity: Castleblayney
Cancer Unit

O'Gorman's **SuperValu** Market Square Shopping
Centre, Carrickmacross t: 042 9661387 Nominated
Charity: Carrickmacross Cancer Fund

Fleming's **SuperValu** The Diamond, Monaghan
t: 047 81344 Nominated Charity: Monaghan Branch
of Special Olympics

## Offaly

Flynn's **SuperValu** Banagher Town Centre, Main
Street, Banagher t: 057 9151516
Nominated Charity: Special Olympics

Buckley's **SuperValu** Main Street, Birr
t: 057 9120015 St. Nominated Charity: St. Vincent
de Paul

## Roscommon

Kelly's **SuperValu** Elphin Street, Boyle
t: 071 9664123 Nominated Charity: Lourdes
Invalid Fund

Cahill's **SuperValu** Main Street, Castlerea
t: 094 9620373 Nominated Charity: St. Michael's
Special School

Fleming's **SuperValu** Main Street, Roscommon
t: 090 6626196 Nominated Charity: Roscommon
Brothers of Charity Services

Smith's **SuperValu** Unit3/4, Rivervillage, Monksland,
Athlone. t: 090 6490022 Nominated Charity:
St. Vincent de Paul

## Sligo

Davey's **SuperValu** Lord Edward Street, Ballymote
t: 071 9183315 Nominated Charity: Sligo Hospice

Surlis' **SuperValu** Teeling Street, Tubbercurry
t: 071 9185096 Nominated Charity: Gallagher House
Resource Centre Tubbercurry

## Tipperary

Caulfield's **SuperValu** Bank Place, Tipperary
t: 062 52930 Nominated Charity: Tipperary
South Hospice

Dolan's **SuperValu** Bridge Street, Cahir t: 052 41515
Nominated Charity: Local St. Vincent de Paul and
Meals on Wheels

Murphy's **SuperValu** Greystone Street, Carrick-on-Suir
t: 051 640803 Nominated Charity: Local St. Vincent
de Paul Society

Tipperary Co-op **SuperValu** Kickham Place, Tipperary
Town t: 062 51901 Nominated Charity: Tipperary
South Hospice

Morrissey's **SuperValu** Main Street, Cashel
t: 062 61555 Nominated Charity: SouthTipperary
Hospice, Cashel

Bernie's **SuperValu** Main Street, Roscrea
t: 0505 21736 Nominated Charity: Sisters of Sacred
Heart of Jesus and Mary

Jones' **SuperValu** Poppyfield, Clonmel t: 052 83522
Nominated Charity: Cuan Saor

Murphy's **SuperValu** Springfield Retail Park, Limerick
Rd, Nenagh t: 067 37260 Nominated Charity:
St. Vincent de Paul

## Waterford

Kelleher's **SuperValu** Cappoquin t: 058 54594
Nominated Charity: West Waterford Hospice

Morrissey's **SuperValu** O' Connell Street, Dungarvan
t: 058 41754 Nominated Charity: Friends of
St. Joseph's Hospice, Dungarvan

Quish's **SuperValu** Priests Road, Tramore
t: 051 386036 Nominated Charity: Meals on
Wheels, Tramore

Caulfield's **SuperValu** The Hypermarket,
Morgan Street t: 051 872028 Nominated Charity:
Lions Club

Garvey's **SuperValu** The Quay, Dungarvan
t: 058 41628 Nominated Charity: Friends of
St. Joseph's Hospice, Dungarvan

## Westmeath

Buckley's **SuperValu** Austin Friars Street, Mullingar
t: 044 9342420 Nominated Charity: St. Finbar's
Community Centre

Bagnall's **SuperValu** Main Street, Kinnegad
t: 044 9375800 Nominated Charity: Saplings Autistic
School, Mullingar

Buckley's **SuperValu** Main Street, Moate
t: 090 6481880 Nominated Charity:
St. Vincent de Paul

## Wexford

Caulfield's **SuperValu** Abbey Street, Enniscorthy
t: 053 9234541 Nominated Charity: Arthritis Ireland
in the South East

Crowe's **SuperValu** Keywest, Custom House Quay,
Wexford Town t: 053 9122290 Nominated Charity:
Friends of Wexford Hospital

Pettitt's **SuperValu** Main Street, Gorey
t: 053 9421506 Nominated Charity: St. Aidan's Day
Care Centre, Gorey

Murphy's **SuperValu** Rosslare Harbour
t: 053 9133107 Nominated Charity: RNLI Rosslare
Harbour

Pettitt's **SuperValu** St Aidans Shopping Centre,
Wexford Town t: 053 9124055 Nominated Charity:
Friends of Wexford General - Cancer Day Care
Unit Appeal

Pettitt's **SuperValu** The Duffry, Enniscorthy
t: 053 9234265 Nominated Charity: St. Vincent
de Paul Enniscourthy

Caulfield's **SuperValu** The Quay, New Ross
t: 051 421392 Nominated Charity: CBS
Primary School

Wallace's **SuperValu** Wellington Bridge
t: 051 561113 Nominated Charity: Friends of
Wexford Hospital

## Wicklow

Daly's **SuperValu** Church Road, Greystones
t: 01 2873900 Nominated Charity: Greystones
Cancer Support

Kenny's **SuperValu** Main Street, Blessington
t: 045 865338 Nominated Charity: Blessington
Life Boat

Gillespie's **SuperValu** Mill Street, Baltinglass
t: 059 6481355 Nominated Charity: West Wicklow
Day Care Centre

Gallagher's **SuperValu** Wentworth Street, Wicklow
Town t: 0404 61888 Nominated Charity:
Wicklow Hospital

Pettitt's **SuperValu** Wexford Road, Arklow
t: 0402 39770 Nominated Charity: Irish Wheelchair
Association, Arklow